W9-AGH-932

WITHDRAWN

1st EDITION

Perspectives on Diseases and Disorders

Food-Borne Diseases

Arthur Gillard

Book Editor

PERSPECTIVES
On Diseases & Disorders

GALE
CENGAGE Learning

Detroit • New York • San Francisco • New Haven, Conn • Waterville, Maine • London

Christine Nasso, *Publisher*
Elizabeth Des Chenes, *Managing Editor*

Articles in Greenhaven Press anthologies are often edited for length to meet page requirements. In addition, original titles of these works are changed to clearly present the main thesis and to explicitly indicate the author's opinion. Every effort is made to ensure that Greenhaven Press accurately reflects the original intent of the authors. Every effort has been made to trace the owners of copyrighted material.

Cover image copyright © Colin Anderson/Photographer's Choice/Getty Images

LIBRARY OF CONGRESS CATALOGING-IN-PUBLICATION DATA

Food-borne diseases / Arthur Gillard, book editor.
   p. cm. -- (Perspectives on diseases and disorders)
  Includes bibliographical references and index.
  ISBN 978-0-7377-5252-6 (hardcover)
  1. Foodborne diseases--Popular works. I. Gillard, Arthur.
  RA601.5.F658 2011
  615.9'54--dc22
                                       2010040081

Printed in the United States of America
1 2 3 4 5 6 7 15 14 13 12 11

CONTENTS

FOREWORD

"Medicine, to produce health, has to examine disease."
—Plutarch

Independent research on a health issue is often the first step to complement discussions with a physician. But locating accurate, well-organized, understandable medical information can be a challenge. A simple Internet search on terms such as "cancer" or "diabetes," for example, returns an intimidating number of results. Sifting through the results can be daunting, particularly when some of the information is inconsistent or even contradictory. The Greenhaven Press series Perspectives on Diseases and Disorders offers a solution to the often overwhelming nature of researching diseases and disorders.

From the clinical to the personal, titles in the Perspectives on Diseases and Disorders series provide students and other researchers with authoritative, accessible information in unique anthologies that include basic information about the disease or disorder, controversial aspects of diagnosis and treatment, and first-person accounts of those impacted by the disease. The result is a well-rounded combination of primary and secondary sources that, together, provide the reader with a better understanding of the disease or disorder.

Each volume in Perspectives on Diseases and Disorders explores a particular disease or disorder in detail. Material for each volume is carefully selected from a wide range of sources, including encyclopedias, journals, newspapers, nonfiction books, speeches, government documents, pamphlets, organization newsletters, and position papers. Articles in the first chapter provide an authoritative, up-to-date overview that covers symptoms, causes and effects, treatments, cures, and medical advances. The second chapter presents a substantial number of opposing viewpoints on controversial treatments and other current debates relating to the volume topic. The third chapter offers a variety of personal perspectives on the disease or disorder. Patients, doctors, caregivers, and loved ones represent just some of the voices found in this narrative chapter.

Each Perspectives on Diseases and Disorders volume also includes:

- An **annotated table of contents** that provides a brief summary of each article in the volume.
- An **introduction** specific to the volume topic.
- Full-color **charts and graphs** to illustrate key points, concepts, and theories.
- Full-color **photos** that show aspects of the disease or disorder and enhance textual material.
- **"Fast Facts"** that highlight pertinent additional statistics and surprising points.
- A **glossary** providing users with definitions of important terms.
- A **chronology** of important dates relating to the disease or disorder.
- An annotated list of **organizations to contact** for students and other readers seeking additional information.
- A **bibliography** of additional books and periodicals for further research.
- A detailed **subject index** that allows readers to quickly find the information they need.

Whether a student researching a disorder, a patient recently diagnosed with a disease, or an individual who simply wants to learn more about a particular disease or disorder, a reader who turns to Perspectives on Diseases and Disorders will find a wealth of information in each volume that offers not only basic information, but also vigorous debate from multiple perspectives.

INTRODUCTION

In 1993, Alexander Thomas Donley, aged six, was one
of four children who died from eating a Jack in the Box
hamburger. *E. coli* O157:H7 first made him curl into a
fetal position from abdominal cramps. Then, one after
another, his organs failed. Screams of pain were followed
by silence as toxins liquefied his brain. He suffered trem-
ors and delusions and finally a massive seizure. His body
swelled as his kidneys shut down. "I was so horrified and
so shocked and so angered by what happened to him,"
says his mother, Nancy Donley, now the president of
Safe Tables Our Priority, or S.T.O.P., a Chicago-based
advocacy group. "I had no idea that there was any problem in our food supply. I loved my child more than anything in this world. And then to find out that he died
because there were contaminated cattle feces in a hamburger. And to find out that had been recognized as a
problem for a while. Why hadn't it been fixed?"[1]

The O157:H7 strain of *E. coli* is an example of an
emerging disease, a new threat that has appeared
on the scene only in the past few decades. But
food-borne diseases have always been with us. Early humans, "like all other predators . . . consumed the sickest
or weakest animals because they were the easiest to kill.
They also ate putrid meat that had been hidden away for
long periods as well as noxious plants or mushrooms. . . .
Most of our prehistoric ancestors generally died in poor
health at an age of twenty to thirty years."[2] Under such
circumstances the scale of suffering and premature death

Shown here is a colored electron micrograph of *E. coli* 0157:H7 bacteria. A food-borne bacterium, *E. coli* produces a powerful toxin that causes abdominal cramps, bloody diarrhea, and sometimes kidney failure. (**Dr. Gary Gaugler/ Photo Researchers, Inc.**)

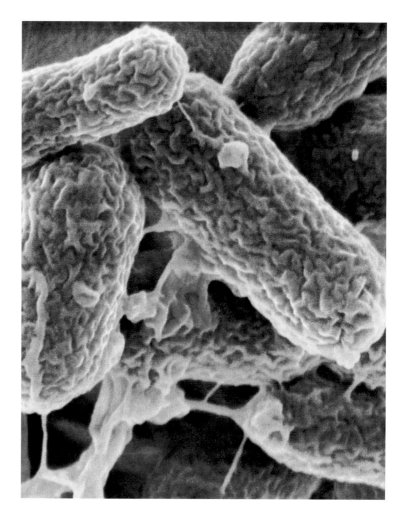

due to food-related illnesses must have been unimaginably horrific.

For most of human history the causes of such diseases were quite mysterious, but starting in the nineteenth century the mechanisms behind such illness began to be understood in detail, and systematic scientific attempts to protect against them became possible, ultimately leading to the formation of organizations such as the Food and Drug Administration (FDA) and increasingly comprehensive regulations that attempted to prevent illness and death caused by toxins and biological pathogens in food.

Ironically, the same scientific and technological advances that led to new means of addressing the age-old problem of food-borne diseases also, paradoxically, brought forth new and improved threats to food safety. The ability to detect adulterants in food went along with a vast increase in the number of adulterants that could be added to food in the first place. Antibiotics were developed to combat infectious diseases, then were given to food animals—who became healthier and more productive as a result—and that unexpectedly led to an increase in antibiotic-resistant food-borne microorganisms. The highly complex industrialized food system that feeds so many people with a minuscule percentage of the labor force has also (some would argue) created conditions under which new diseases such as the deadly strain of *E. coli* that killed Alexander Thomas Donley can evolve. Once such a disease has appeared, the modern food-distribution system enables such a disease to spread far and wide with ease, potentially affecting large numbers of people in a very short time.

Nothing illustrates this paradox of progress so much as the new field of nanotechnology, which deals with materials on a molecular scale and shows great promise in detecting and combating food-borne diseases at the same time as it introduces new risks and challenges to the food safety regulatory system. Many nanotechnology applications are being developed to detect food-borne toxins and pathogens; for example, the company Agro-Micron "has developed the NanoBioluminescence Detection Spray which contains a luminescent protein that has been engineered to bind to the surface of microbes such as *Salmonella* and *E. coli*. When bound, it emits a visible glow, thus allowing easy detection of contaminated food or beverages. The more intense the glow is, the higher the bacterial contamination."[3] Clemson University researchers have used nanoparticles to detect *Campylobacter*, another bacterial cause of food-borne disease, and researchers at Rutgers University are developing an "electronic tongue" consisting of microscopic sensors that can be embedded in food packaging, detecting the gases given off when food spoils, and changing color to indicate the food has gone bad. Current testing for pathogens takes days, so the promise of such techniques' delivering results instantly could make a huge difference in controlling future disease outbreaks.

But for all its promise in enhancing food safety, nanotechnology comes with unique potential hazards as well. Nanoparticles are so tiny that they can easily slip through cell membranes and travel freely throughout the body, a feature that also makes it hard for the body to get rid of them. Further complicating the situation, "at the nano-scale . . . the physical, chemical and biological properties of materials may differ in fundamental ways from the properties of individual atoms, molecules and the well-characterized bulk matter from which the nano-sized particles (NSPs) are derived."[4] For example, the common food additive titanium dioxide is considered very safe and is approved for use by the FDA, even though an increasing number of studies are suggesting that *nano*-titanium dioxide, i.e. titanium dioxide that has been reduced to nanoparticle size, may be harmful because of its changed properties. When molecular biologist Bénédicte Trouiller introduced nano-titanium dioxide to the drinking water of lab mice, she discovered it was destroying the chromosomes and DNA of the animals. Genetic toxicologist Robert Schiestl notes that the type of damage Trouiller discovered has been "linked to all the big killers of man, namely cancer, heart disease, neurological disease and aging."[5]

Despite these dangers, nano-titanium dioxide is already being used in a wide variety of food products. Because the Food and Drug Administration does not differentiate between titanium dioxide and nano-titanium dioxide and because it classifies the conventional form of the chemical under the heading "Generally Recognized as Safe," nano-titanium dioxide effectively slips under the regulatory radar screen, as do many other nano-scale materials already being used in the food system.

The age-old battle against food-borne diseases has reached a complex and fascinating phase, which will require fresh thinking, new approaches, and increased vigilance. New technologies and materials, novel threats, and increased insight into the mechanisms of these diseases will serve to further complicate the already complex issue of food-borne diseases.

In *Perspectives on Diseases and Disorders: Food-Borne Diseases* the contributing authors discuss and debate the causes of and controversies around this timely topic as well as relating some personal experiences of suffering food-borne diseases.

Notes

1. Madeline Drexler, *Emerging Epidemics: The Menace of New Infections.* London: Penguin, 2010, pp. 117–18.
2. Morton Satin, *Death in the Pot: The Impact of Food Poisoning on History.* Amherst, NY: Prometheus Books, 2007, p. 45.
3. Tiju Joseph and Mark Morrison, "Nanotechnology in Agriculture and Food," www.nanoforum.org, May 2006, p. 8. www.acss.ws/News.aspx?id=83.
4. George Burdock and Sabine Teske, "Nanotechnology: Benefits vs. Toxic Risks," *Functional Ingredients,* February 1, 2007, p. 18. www.functionalingredientsmag .com/article/Business-Strategies/nanotechnology-benefits-vs-toxic-risks.aspx.
5. Quoted in Andrew Schneider, "Amid Nanotech's Dazzling Promise, Health Risks Grow," *AOL News,* March 24, 2010. www.aolnews.com/nanotech/article/ amid-nanotechs-dazzling-promise-health-risks-grow/19401235.

CHAPTER 1

Understanding Food-Borne Diseases

An Overview of Food-Borne Diseases

Gordana Ristic

Gordana Ristic is on the faculty of medicine at the Institute of Hygiene and Medical Ecology in Belgrade, Serbia. She holds a doctor of science degree (equivalent to a PhD) in the School of Biology, University of Belgrade. In the following viewpoint Ristic introduces the reader to the various categories of food-borne diseases. Microorganisms are a major source of disease, and the author briefly describes a number of common bacterial health threats, including *E. coli* and *Salmonella*. She explains that viruses and prions (abnormal forms of naturally occurring proteins) can also cause disease, as can chemical contamination (whether natural or artificial). Finally, the author briefly mentions a number of techniques used to make food safer, including hazard analysis and critical control point (HACCP), an organized approach to preventing every possible hazard in the food production process.

SOURCE: Gordana Ristic, "Food Safety," *Encyclopedia of Public Health*, Wilhelm Kirch, ed. Springer, 2008. Copyright © 2008 Springer. Part of Springer Science and Business Media. Reproduced with kind permission from Springer Science and Business Media and the author.

Photo on facing page. Good hygiene on the part of food handlers is essential to food safety. (Glenn Stubbe/ MCT/Landov)

Food safety presents a major health problem in the world. There are more than 250 food-borne diseases registered. Serious outbreaks of food-borne disease have been documented on every continent every year, illustrating the public health and social significance of this problem. Food-borne diseases may affect all levels of the population, but the most susceptible are children, pregnant women, the elderly, and those with chronic diseases. Modern farming methods, globalization of the food trade and the higher accessibility of food produce a challenge for food safety and the prevention of the spread of food contaminants worldwide. Food safety programs are focusing on the farm-to-table approach as an effective means of reducing food-borne hazards. Hazards may emerge from microbiological, chemical or physical contamination of food. Health significance of these hazards is estimated through risk assessment method, and thus hazards are regulated, controlled and kept under surveillance.

Microbiological Hazards

Food-borne diseases caused by microorganisms present a major health issue. The most frequent infections are caused by [bacteria such as] *Escherichia coli, Salmonella, Campylobacter jejuni, Listeria monocytogenes;* parasites like *cryptosporidium, cryptospora, trematodes;* and viruses. According to WHO [World Health Organization] data almost 1.8 million children die each year in developing countries (excluding China) from diarrhoeal disease caused by microbes which are present in food and water. In the USA each year some 100 million cases are attributed to food-borne illnesses, resulting in 325,000 hospitalizations and about 5000 deaths. Health experts estimate that the yearly cost of all food-borne diseases in the USA is 5 to 6 billion dollars in direct medical expenses and lost productivity. Infections with the bacteria *Salmonella* alone account for $1 billion yearly in direct and indirect medical costs.

Five most frequent food-borne diseases are:
- Botulism
- Campylobacteriosis
- *E. coli* infection
- Salmonellosis
- Shigellosis

Botulism is a disease caused by *Bacillus botulinum,* an agent emerging from soil. The most common sources are canned meat and vegetables and the production of toxin can be regulated by controlling the acid pH of food.

Campylobacteriosis is an infectious disease caused by *Campylobacter* bacteria. *Campylobacter jejuni, C. fetus,*

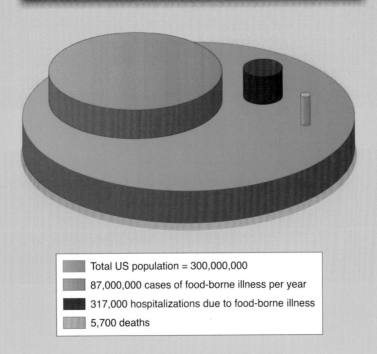

Causes of Food-Borne Diseases in the United States, per Year

Total US population = 300,000,000

87,000,000 cases of food-borne illness per year

317,000 hospitalizations due to food-borne illness

5,700 deaths

Taken from: Mike Stobbe, "Food-Borne Illnesses Hit Plateau in U.S.," *Washington Times*, April 10, 2009.

and *C. coli* are the types that usually cause campylobacteriosis in people. *C. jejuni* causes most cases of the illness. Infection can be caused by handling raw poultry, eating undercooked poultry, drinking nonchlorinated water or raw milk, or handling infected animal or human feces. Most frequently, poultry and cattle waste are the sources of the bacteria, but feces from puppies, kittens, and birds also may be contaminated.

E. coli and Salmonella

Escherichia coli infection is caused by different strains of *E. coli* bacteria. Harmless strains of *E. coli* can be found widely in nature, including the intestinal tracts of humans and warm-blooded animals. Disease-causing strains, however, are a frequent cause of both intestinal and urinary-genital tract infections. Several different strains of harmful *E. coli* can cause diarrheal disease. A particularly dangerous type is called enterohemorrhagic *E. coli*, or EHEC. EHEC often causes bloody diarrhea and can lead to kidney failure in children or people with weakened immune systems.

In 1982, scientists identified the first dangerous strain in the United States. The type of harmful *E. coli* most commonly found in this country is named O157:H7, which refers to chemical compounds found on the bacterium's surface. This type produces one or more related, powerful toxins which can severely damage the lining of the intestines. This strain is now found worldwide and presents one of the most toxic bacterial sources to be found in food and water.

Salmonellosis, is usually provoked by *Salmonella typhimurium* and *S. enteritidis*. *Salmonella* bacteria can be found in food products such as raw poultry, eggs, and beef, and sometimes on unwashed fruit. Food prepared on surfaces that previously were in contact with raw meat or meat products can, in turn, become contaminated with the bacteria. This is called cross-contamination.

With the spread of organic farming new cases are recorded from eating raw alfalfa sprouts grown in contaminated soil. *Salmonella* infection frequently occurs after handling pets.

Shigella and *Listeria*

Shigellosis, also called bacillary dysentery, is an infectious disease caused by *Shigella* bacteria. Four main types of *Shigella* cause infection: *Shigella dysenteriae, S. flexneri, S. boydii*, and *S. sonnei*. It is commonly transmitted by food service workers who are sick or infected, but have no symptoms, and who do not properly wash their hands after using the toilet.

Listeria monocytogenes is a bacterium that can cause a serious infection in humans called listeriosis. Food-borne illness caused by *L. monocytogenes* in pregnant women can result in miscarriage, fetal death, and severe illness

An electron micrograph of *Listeria monocytogenes* shows the food-borne bacteria as blue rod shapes. Listeriosis can cause meningitis and encephalitis. **(Martin Oeggerli/Photo Researchers, Inc.)**

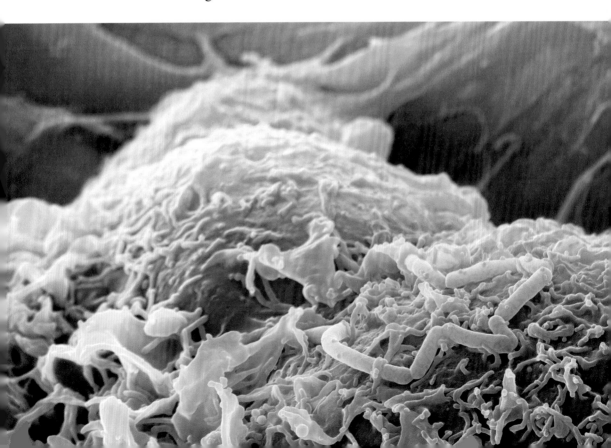

or death of a newborn infant. Others at risk for severe illness or death are older adults and those with weakened immune systems. Listeriosis is now attributed to ready-to-eat foods and deli products.

Food-Borne Viruses and Prions

Diarrhea can be caused by viruses present in food and water such as: caliciviruses, rotavirus, astrovirus, and hepatitis A virus. Norwalk virus (a particular calicivirus) caused a number of outbreaks of food poisoning at buffets and caterings. Current studies are trying to produce new vaccines, including edible vaccines against Norwalk virus and hepatitis. Recently, an inactivated vaccine for hepatitis A virus infection has been developed. Mad Cow Disease is the commonly used name for bovine spongiform encephalopathy (BSE), a slowly progressive, degenerative, fatal disease affecting the central nervous system of adult cattle. The exact cause of BSE is not known but it is generally accepted by the scientific community that the likely cause is infectious forms of a type of protein, prions, normally found in animals. In cattle with BSE, these abnormal prions initially occur in the small intestines and tonsils, and are found in central nervous tissues, such as the brain and spinal cord, and other tissues of infected animals experiencing later stages of the disease. There is a disease similar to BSE called Creutzfeldt-Jakob Disease (CJD) that is found in people. A variant form of CJD (vCJD) is believed to be caused by eating contaminated beef products from BSE-affected cattle. To date [as of 2008], there have been 155 confirmed and probable cases of vCJD worldwide.

Other Causes of Food-Borne Disease

Chemicals are a significant source of food-borne diseases, but it is sometimes difficult to link them to particular food. Chemicals include: natural toxicants such as mycotoxins and marine toxins, environmental contaminants such as mercury, lead, radionuclides and dioxins, but, also, naturally occurring chemicals in plants, such as glycoalkaloids in potatoes. Migration from packaging material has also been investigated, and Acrylamide, as a chemical compound that migrates, is widely studied. Food additives and nutrients such as vitamins and minerals, pesticides and veterinary drug residues are used deliberately in order to increase food supply, but assurance that they are safe must be obtained prior to their use. Chemical contaminants may affect health through single use, but most commonly they act after long-term exposure. Risk assessment must be performed in order to assess the potential for causing diseases after exposure to chemicals in food and water.

> **FAST FACT**
>
> According to the World Health Organization, about 1.8 million people around the world died from diarrhea-related diseases in 2005; a large percentage of diarrhea cases result from contaminated food and water.

Genetic engineering, irradiation of food, ohmic [electrical] heating and modified atmosphere packaging are used to increase agricultural production, extend shelf life or make food safer. Potential for causing food allergies should be carefully examined, as well as other possible changes. Food produced from or using genetically modified organisms (GMO) must be proven to be equivalent to conventionally produced food in terms of nutritional value and safety.

Control of Food Safety

Control over food safety must be performed through the whole food chain. It combines good agricultural practices (GAP) in basic production of food commodities, with good manufacturing practices (GMP) and standard sanitary operating procedures (SSOP) in food processing premises. The best way of controlling hazards in food production proved to be hazard analysis and critical control point (HACCP)—a preventive approach to identification and control of all possible hazards to be found in production of a certain foodstuff.

Access to safe food is one of the basic human rights. In spite of this, food-borne diseases still present major health problems both in developing and industrialized countries. Contaminants may be naturally occurring, but due to new agricultural techniques and demands for certain qualities and extended shelf-life of products, new pathogens are discovered along with classic ones. A holistic approach to food safety requires control of potential hazards throughout the food chain and this preventative approach should be fostered instead of the classic method of spot checking and analyzing of final products.

Food-Borne Diseases Are a Significant Problem in the Developing World

World Health Organization

The World Health Organization (WHO) is the directing and coordinating authority for health within the United Nations. It provides leadership on global health matters, provides technical support to countries, and monitors and assesses health trends. In the following viewpoint WHO notes that food-borne diseases are a problem throughout the world, but the developing world is affected much more strongly due to a greater prevalence of the factors leading to food-borne diseases, such as poor sanitation and contaminated environments. In addition, the report says that developing countries are less able to deal with the effects of food-borne illness, due to inadequate treatment facilities and other issues. Despite the magnitude of this problem, there is very little accurate and up-to-date information available on these diseases in the developing world, which has led WHO to launch initiatives to gather much-needed data.

SOURCE: World Health Organization, "Summary Document: WHO Initiative to Estimate the Global Burden of Foodborne Diseases," www.who.int/en/, 2008. Reproduced by permission.

Food safety touches all our lives. Meat, eggs, fish, but also chocolate, peanut butter and lettuce—all of these products have been associated with contamination and foodborne illness. New foodborne as well as antibiotic-resistant pathogens have emerged which are circumventing conventional control measures. In many parts of the world, foodborne diseases are appearing to increase and problems in one part of the world are now quickly exported. Yet no global estimation of the disease burden has ever been performed, with the exception of a few national studies that have examined microbial incidence of foodborne diseases.

A Leading Cause of Death Worldwide

Foodborne diseases are an important cause of morbidity and mortality worldwide. Diarrhoeal diseases alone—a considerable proportion of which is foodborne—kill 1.9 million children globally every year. Although most of these diarrhoeal deaths occur in poor countries, foodborne diseases are not limited to developing countries. It is estimated that in the United States, foodborne diseases result in 76 million illnesses, 325,000 hospitalizations and 5,000 deaths each year. The full extent of the burden and cost of unsafe food, however, is currently unknown. Data from developing countries, where populations are particularly exposed to contaminated environments, are scarce. Precise information on the burden of disease is needed to adequately inform policy-makers how best to allocate resources for appropriate foodborne disease control efforts. Without concerted action to estimate and reduce the burden of foodborne diseases, global health security will be jeopardized and international efforts to achieve the Millennium Development Goals [set by the United Nations], including the overarching goal of poverty reduction, will be impaired. In 2006 and in collaboration with multiple international partners, WHO's Department of Food Safety, Zoonoses and

Foodborne Diseases (FOS) held an international consultation to launch an initiative and provide a strategic framework to estimate the global burden of foodborne diseases. One of the consultation's main recommendations was to establish—under the leadership of WHO/FOS—a multi-disciplinary Foodborne Disease Burden Epidemiology Reference Group (FERG) to implement the consultation's strategic recommendations and estimate the global burden of foodborne diseases. . . .

A Greater Impact on the Developing World

In today's interconnected world, local foodborne disease outbreaks potentially affect the entire globe. Originating in East Asia, the H5N1 bird flu virus has spread to many parts of the world. Baby corn exported from Thailand recently led to *Shigellosis* outbreaks in Australia and Denmark, and frozen dumplings imported from China led to *organo-phosphate* poisoning of more than 3,000 consumers in Japan, with many of them requiring hospital care. These examples demonstrate our universal vulnerability and the threat that *food contamination poses to public health security*.

Concerns about food safety have skyrocketed in more affluent societies. Food scares involving *Salmonella* and *E. Coli O157:H7* in the United States or the spread of *bovine spongiform encephalopathy (BSE)* [mad cow disease] in Europe were prominently featured in the media and have alarmed consumers. However, the *real tragedy of foodborne diseases is played out in the developing world.* Unsafe water used for the cleaning and processing of food, poor food-production processes and handling (including inappropriate use of agricultural chemicals), the absence of adequate food storage infrastructure and inadequate or poorly enforced regulatory standards all

> ## FAST FACT
>
> Each year, more children die from diarrhea, often caused by contaminated food, than from AIDS, malaria, and measles combined, according to a 2009 World Health Organization report.

contribute to a high risk environment. Moreover, as a country's economy develops, the agricultural landscape changes. Intensive animal husbandry practices are put in place to maximize production resulting in the increased prevalence of pathogens such as *Salmonella* and *Campylobacter* in flocks and herds. The tropical climate of many developing countries favours the proliferation of pests and naturally occurring toxins, and the risk of contracting parasitic diseases, including worm infestations.

While exposed to more hazardous environments, *people in developing countries often have difficulty coping with foodborne diseases.* For many living at/below the poverty line, food-borne illness perpetuates the cycle of poverty. The symptoms of foodborne diseases range from mild and self-limiting (nausea, vomiting and diarrhoea) to debilitating and life-threatening symptoms (such as kidney and liver failure, brain and neural disorders, paralysis and potentially cancers) leading to long periods of absenteeism and death. Without substantial investment in food safety prevention and control the achievement of the Millennium Development Goal (MDG) 1 which aims to *eradicate global monetary poverty and reduce hunger by 2015, will be jeopardized.* Detailed data on the economic costs of foodborne diseases in developing countries are largely missing. In the United States, a government report estimated in 1993 that foodborne diseases account for up to USD [U.S. dollars] 9.4 billion in lost work and medical expenses annually. On the basis of per capita income, the economic burden to people in India affected by an outbreak of *Staphylococcus aureus* food poisoning was estimated to be higher than the costs resulting from a similar outbreak in the US.

Undermine Economic Development

Foodborne pathogens take advantage of weak immune systems. Infants and young children, pregnant women, the elderly as well as immuno-compromised people are

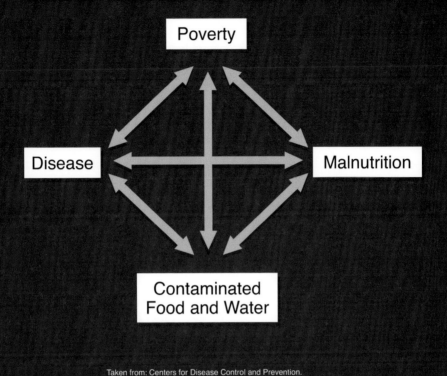

Poor Nations Endure a Vicious Cycle

Poverty

Disease

Malnutrition

Contaminated
Food and Water

Taken from: Centers for Disease Control and Prevention.

particularly at risk of contracting and dying from common food-related diseases. Every year, 1.9 million children die of diarrhoeal disease, an illness which is generally easy to treat. Malnourished infants and children are especially exposed to foodborne hazards and are at higher risk of developing serious forms of foodborne diarrhoeal diseases; these infections in turn exacerbate malnutrition thus leading to a vicious circle and mortality. Those who survive may suffer from delayed physical and mental development, depriving them of the opportunity to reach their full potential in society. It is unlikely that the internationally agreed goal of *reducing child mortality by two thirds* will be achieved unless countries recognize the need for and invest in improvements in domestic food safety.

Beyond the individual level, *foodborne diseases affect economic development*, particularly challenging the tourist, agricultural and food (export) industry. Developing countries' access to food export markets will depend on their capacity to meet the international regulatory requirements determined by the Agreement on the Application of Sanitary and Phylosanitary Measures (SPS) of the World Trade Organization (WTO). Unsafe exports can lead to significant economic losses as shown in early 2008, when Indian poultry products valued at several hundred thousand USD were refused entry to Saudi Arabia and remained stranded on ships in the Persian Gulf and Arabian Sea, following a bird flu outbreak in the Indian state of West Bengal.

In recent years, a new understanding of the importance of foodborne diseases has emerged. Since the Uruguay Round of Multilateral Trade Negotiations in 1994, international attention has focused on ensuring compliance with international norms and standards for food exports. In 2000, the World Health Assembly (WHA) of the World Health Organization (WHO) adopted WHA Resolution 53.15 on Food Safety, acknowledging foodborne diseases as a widespread and growing threat to health in all countries. In 2007 and in recognition of the growing threat posed by foodborne diseases worldwide, over 50 developed and developing countries adopted the Beijing Declaration on Food Safety at a high-level International Forum. The Declaration urges all countries to base their food safety measures on sound scientific evidence and risk analysis.

Despite the growing international awareness of foodborne diseases as a significant risk to health and socio-economic development, food safety remains marginalized. A major obstacle to adequately addressing food safety concerns is the lack of accurate data on the full extent and cost of foodborne diseases, which would enable policy makers to set public health priorities and

allocate resources. Epidemiological data on foodborne diseases remain scarce, particularly in the developing world. Even the most visible foodborne outbreaks often go unrecognized, unreported or uninvestigated and may only be visible if connected to major public health or economic impact.

In 2007 the World Health Organization held a forum in China to discuss food safety problems in the developing world. (Kyoda/AP Images)

Ergotism Is a Fungal Food-Borne Disease

Morton Satin

Morton Satin is a molecular biologist, former director of the United Nations Food and Agriculture Organization's Global Agribusiness Program, and author of *Food Alert! The Ultimate Sourcebook for Food Safety*. In the following excerpts Satin discusses ergot, a fungus that infects common cereals. As Satin explains, when humans eat ergot-infected grains, the result is either gangrenous ergotism, in which people experience extreme heat followed by gangrene (tissue death) and loss of fingers, toes, or limbs; or victims may experience convulsive ergotism, resulting in symptoms such as numbness, irritability, or hallucinations. Satin says that during the Middle Ages the gangrenous ergotism was known as St. Anthony's Fire after a nobleman and his son experienced being cured of ergotism, which cure they attributed to St. Anthony. According to Satin, there have been many outbreaks throughout history, including a case in A.D. 944 in which up to forty thousand people died, as well as an outbreak in a French village in 1951 in which hundreds of people went mad after eating bread made from infected grain.

Most people have never heard of ergotism, much less the mold that causes it, *Claviceps purpurea*. This fungus starts life out as a small, black rind-covered tube called a sclerotium. Barely more than half an inch long and an eighth of an inch wide, this harmless-looking tube is easily mistaken for a broken piece of plant stalk and would likely go totally unnoticed lying on the winter ground. Within its thick walls, however, a compact mass of mycelium [fungal "roots"] lies dormant, awaiting the proper time to awake.

Ergot Infects Common Cereals

With the arrival of spring, the sclerotium awakens and sprouts a dozen or more stalks that looked like tiny enoki mushrooms. The heads of these stalks produce and discharge spores that are light enough to be carried by the passing winds. If they land on cereals, they quickly colonize them and produce a new sclerotium at every infection site.

Because the sclerotia resemble the spur of a rooster's leg, they were called "ergot" by the French.

The cereals most commonly affected are wheat, barley, rye, and oats—all common staples of the Western diet. . . . It would be quite easy to harvest the sclerotium along with the rest of the grain. According to agricultural records, in cold, damp periods, as much as a quarter of the harvest could be made up of ergot sclerotia! (Fortunately, this is no longer a significant problem because of improved post-harvest practices and access to hot-air drying.)

Manually culling out these contaminants is a very time-consuming job, and it is not surprising that a considerable amount of ergot eventually becomes mixed in with the rest of the cereal grains. What makes matters worse is that the *Claviceps* continues to thrive if the moisture content exceeds 14 percent—a situation not uncommon in grain storage. Once the grain is removed from storage and milled into flour, it is very difficult to tell that

Ergot fungus is shown replacing grain in ripe wheat. The most commonly infected cereal grains are wheat, barley, rye, and oats. (**Nigel Cattlin/ Photo Researchers, Inc.**)

a product is toxic. Aside from some slight discoloration, ergot-contaminated flour looks exactly like normal flour.

Ergot Affects the Central Nervous System

Ergot toxins are alkaloids (nitrogenous plant chemicals) that have profound effects on the central nervous system. Many of them are very powerful hallucinogens, including lysergic acid diethylamide, more commonly known as LSD. Aside from causing hallucinations, these toxins can severely contract arteries (vasoconstrictor) and smooth muscles, causing numbness, extreme sensitivity, and irritability.

In ancient times, the Chinese, Greeks, and Romans actually used ergot for its medicinal properties. A tea-like infusion from infected rye was used to reduce or stop postpartum hemorrhaging or to stop the bleeding of severe wounds. The vasoconstrictor function of the alkaloid ergotamine was even used to induce abortions. As a result, whenever flour contaminated with ergot was consumed unknowingly, the odds of miscarriage were increased enormously.

Ergotism manifests itself in two distinct ways. The first is called gangrenous ergotism, and the second is known as convulsive ergotism. Sometimes, both conditions can be found in the same victim.

Historically, gangrenous ergotism is more prominent, having been responsible for the infamous affliction St. Anthony's Fire. In this terrible manifestation of ergot-induced vasoconstriction, the limbs and their extremities (fingers and toes) become swollen and highly inflamed. Victims experience sensations of extreme heat (the "Holy Fire"). Within a few weeks, gangrene sets in and the fingers, toes, or limbs become necrotic [dead] and fall off. As can be imagined, this whole process was agonizingly painful because the limbs felt like they were consumed by fire.

Ergotism Outbreaks Have Occurred for Millennia

Ergotism has been a regular curse to rye- and other grain-eating populations for millennia. It was first described in an Assyrian tablet as a "noxious pustule in the ear of grain." The ancient Egyptians were aware of a disease caused by eating certain grains that produced both convulsions and hallucinations. In 875 CE [of the common era, aka A.D.], the "Annals of Xanthes" described how "a great plague of swollen blisters consumed the people by a loathsome rot so that their limbs were loosened and fell off before death." It was the first report of a mass outbreak of ergotism.

Another European ergot epidemic appeared in the eleventh century and was christened *ignis sacer* (Latin for "holy fire"). Although less common in England than in the rest of Europe, a number of major outbreaks of ergotism were recorded there in 1762 and 1734. In Russia, ergotism was a major health hazard, particularly in times of famine when little choice was left but to consume even blighted grain.

Important Mycotoxins That Have Been Found in Some Agricultural Food Commodities

Mycotoxin	Major fungal species	Major foods involved
Aflatoxins B_1, B_2, G_1, G_2	A. flavus A. parasiticus A. nomius	Peanuts, maize, cottonseeds
Aflatoxins M_1, M_2	Metabolites of aflatoxins B_1, B_2	Milk and dairy products
Patulin	P. expansum	Apple juice and apple-related products
Ochratoxin A	P. verrucosum A. ochraceus	Cereals, legumes, coffee beans
Fumonisin B_1	F. moniliforme F. proliferatum	Maize
Trichothecenes	F. sporotrichiodes F. poae F. graminearum F. culmorum	Cereals, maize
Zearalenone	F. graminearum F. culmorum F. crookwellense	Maize

Taken from: Food and Environmental Hygiene Department, Government of the Hong Kong Special Administrative Region.

Out of desperation, victims prayed to their various saints for relief. One of the most popular saints was St. Anthony. Born in Alexandria, Egypt, in 251 CE, Anthony came from a wealthy family. At a young age, he gave all his wealth to the poor and banished himself to the desert where he became a hermit. He eventually migrated to Europe where he lived to the ripe old age of 105.

The Origin of "St. Anthony's Fire"

After his death, Anthony was secretly buried on his mountain retreat. However, in the year 561, his remains were discovered and moved back to Alexandria. After the city was sacked by Saracens in 1070, his remains were transferred to Constantinople (Istanbul). When the city was captured by the Crusaders, the emperor of Constantinople presented a member of the French nobility the remains of St. Anthony, which were promptly transported to the church of La Motte near Vienne, France.

In 1089 there was a terrible plague of ergotism in the French town of La Motte. A nobleman and his son were among those stricken, but in time, both were miraculously cured by what they believed were the magical powers of the ancient relics of St. Anthony housed in their local church. The nobleman, Gaston, and his son, Girond, soon pledged themselves and their estate to establish a hospital near the church. Since that time, gangrenous ergotism, previously called the Holy Fire, became commonly known as St. Anthony's Fire.

More than one hundred major outbreaks of St. Anthony's Fire have been reported with as many as forty thousand deaths attributed to a single incident that occurred in the year 944 in France. Despite our knowledge of the disease and the toxins that cause it, we continue to experience outbreaks. In the twentieth century, at least four major outbreaks occurred in the Soviet Union (1926), Ireland (1929), France (1951), and Ethiopia (1978).

A Terrible Outbreak in France

The 1951 outbreak occurred in the small French village of Pont St. Esprit. This tiny town took its name from the old bridge that spanned the Rhône River. That year, France experienced one of its wettest summers in a very long time. The conditions were ideal for the development of *Claviceps*, and in mid-August, one of the town's two bakers noticed that the new batch of flour he used to make his baguettes [long, thin loaves of French bread] was slightly grayer than the flour he normally used. Since flour distribution was a government monopoly at the time, he felt he had no choice but to use the flour he was given.

Within a day, more than two hundred of the villagers, all of whom purchased his baguettes, became very ill with what appeared to be food poisoning. Several people began to complain of lightheadedness, nausea, vomiting, vertigo, and diarrhea. In spite of the village's typical summer heat, people felt like they were freezing. Soon, people started going berserk, screaming through the night that they were being attacked by terrible apparitions. The hallucinations made people jump out of windows, claiming that they were on fire or that they could fly like airplanes.

The likely cause of this was the baguettes made with ergot-contaminated flour. Symptoms of both the gangrenous and the convulsive forms of ergotism combined to produce an epidemic that was so bizarre and frightening that the outbreak captured the French newspaper headlines for weeks. It took some time before the consulting physicians brought in to analyze the problem noticed a resemblance between the ongoing difficulties in the town and epidemics of ergot poisoning that had occurred more than a century before. Others, including the police, thought that they were witnessing some form of

> **FAST FACT**
>
> Research suggests that some of the women and girls tried in the Salem witch trials of 1692 may have been suffering hallucinations due to the effects of convulsive ergotism.

mercury contamination—akin to Mad Hatter's disease. But the laboratory data eventually pointed to ergotism.

Before this incident ebbed, hundreds of villagers suffered weeks of unbearable sleeplessness and hallucinations. Four of them died agonizing deaths. It was months before the village of Pont St. Esprit returned to a semblance of normal life. The memory of *le pain maudit* (the accursed bread) still remains.

The Evolution of
E. coli O157:H7

Madeline Drexler

Madeline Drexler is a journalist specializing in medicine, science, and public health. She is the editor of the *Harvard Public Health Review* and author of *Emerging Epidemics: The Menace of New Infections.* In the following viewpoint Drexler describes the evolutionary history of *E. coli* O157:H7, a particularly deadly strain of *E. coli* which has caused a number of deadly outbreaks. According to Drexler, *E. coli* normally helps keep humans healthy by keeping disease-causing bacteria in the intestines at acceptable levels; however, the O157:H7 strain has itself evolved into a deadly form. Drexler explains that this strain became dangerous by acquiring the ability to produce the third most deadly bacterial toxin, known as Shiga toxin, as well as developing an increased acid-resistance, so that it is able to survive better in the human stomach. The author says that the strain has been around for a long time, but changes in human activity, such as industrial meat production, have provided it the opportunity to thrive in the modern world.

SOURCE: Madeline Drexler, *Emerging Epidemics: The Menace of New Infections.* Washington, DC: Joseph Henry Press, 2010. Reprinted with permission from the National Academies Press, Copyright 2010, National Academy of Sciences.

Every pathogen has a story, but the biography of *E. coli* O157:H7 is especially instructive because it shows how chance favors the prepared germ—and how we are giving certain disease-causing organisms more chances [to thrive] than a rigged roulette wheel. Though *E. coli* O157:H7 has turned up in unpasteurized apple cider in 1991, 1996, and nearly every year since the [natural juice company] Odwalla outbreak [in 1998], it is best known as the agent behind "hamburger disease." Hamburgers, in fact, are Rolls-Royce conveyances for O157. Think of your next Big Mac as the end product of a vast on-the-hoof assembly line. The story begins on hundreds of feedlots in different states and foreign countries. The animals are shuttled to slaughterhouses, where they become carcasses. The carcasses go to plants that separate meat from bone. The boning plants ship giant bins of meat to hamburger-making plants. The hamburger-making plants combine meat from many different bins to make raw hamburgers. At this point, your burger is more fluid than solid, because ground beef continually mixes and flows as it's made, its original ingredients indistinguishable. Grinding also multiplies surface area, so that the meat becomes a kind of soup or lab medium for bacteria. Finally, from the hamburger-making plants, these mongrel patties are frozen and sent to restaurants. A single patty may mingle the meat of a hundred different animals from four different countries. Or, looked at from another perspective, a single contaminated carcass shredded for hamburger can pollute eight tons of finished ground beef. Finding the source of contamination becomes impossibly daunting. (Making juice is also like making hamburgers: one bad apple can ruin a huge batch.) In the [fast-food chain] Jack in the Box outbreak [in 1993], investigators found that the ground beef from the most likely supplier contained meat from 443 different cattle that had come from farms and auction in six states via five slaughterhouses. As the meat industry consolidates and the size of ground beef lots grows, a single carcass may have even more deadly potential. In 1997, Hudson Foods was forced to recall 25 million pounds of ground beef for this very reason: a small part of one day's contaminated beef lot was mistakenly mixed with the next day's, vastly spreading the risk.

A Deadly *E. coli* Strain Emerges

E. coli O157:H7, the organism that this endless mixing amplifies, is a quiet tenant in the intestines of the 50 percent or so of feedlot cattle it infects, but a vicious hooligan in the human gut. In the bowel, *Escherichia coli*, rod-shaped bacteria first described by German pediatrician Theodore Escherich in 1885, perform a vital task by keeping disease-causing bacteria from taking over. For many decades, that knowledge obscured the fact that some forms of *E. coli* trigger violent disease. *E. coli* O157:H7 (the letters and numbers refer to immune system-provoking antigens on the body and on the whiplike flagella of the organism) was discovered in 1982, during an epidemic spread by undercooked patties from McDonald's restaurants in Oregon and Michigan. The outbreak wasn't highly publicized; even some scientists perceived O157 as more of an academic curiosity than a harbinger of bad things. Eleven years later, the Jack in the Box hamburger chain promoted its "Monster Burgers" with the tag line: "So good it's scary." These large, too-lightly-grilled patties killed four children and sickened more than 700 people—bringing the exotic-sounding bacterium out of the lab and into public consciousness. In fact, however, by the time of the Jack in the Box tragedy, 22 outbreaks of *E. coli* O157:H7, killing 35 people, had already been documented in the United States. Suddenly, fast food hamburgers—a staple of American culture—were potentially lethal.

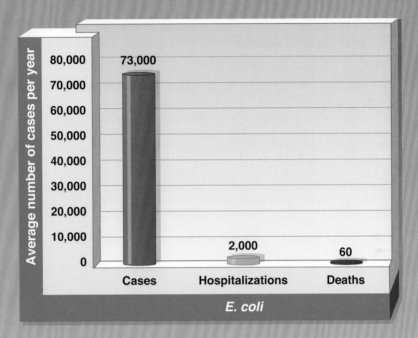

E. coli O157:H7 in the United States

Average number of cases per year

Cases	73,000
Hospitalizations	2,000
Deaths	60

E. coli

Taken from: *Food Poison Journal*, October 31, 2009.

The Virulent Shiga Toxin

What makes *E. coli* O157:H7 so fearsome is the poison it churns out—the third most deadly bacterial toxin, after those causing tetanus and botulism. Known as a Shiga toxin, because it is virtually identical to the toxin produced by *Shigella dysenteriae* type 1, it is a major killer in developing nations. The distinctive symptoms of *E. coli* O157:H7 are bloody diarrhea and fierce abdominal cramps; many victims say it's the worst pain they ever suffered, comparing it to a hot poker searing their insides. Between 2 and 7 percent of patients—mostly young children and the elderly—develop hemolytic uremic syndrome [HUS], which can lead to death. HUS sets in when Shiga toxins ravage the cells lining the intestines. The bleeding that ensues permits the toxins to

A light micrograph of a section of a small intestine shows *E. coli* O157:H7–produced shiga toxin in green. Shiga toxin is the third deadliest bacterial toxin. **(Stephanie Schuller/Photo Researchers, Inc.)**

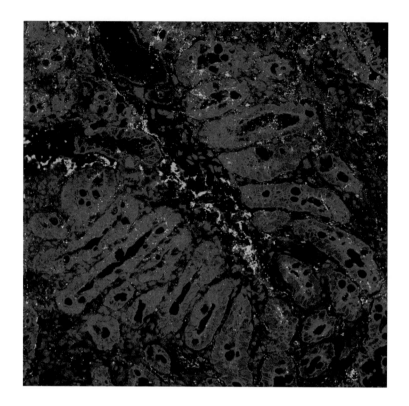

stream into the circulatory system, setting up a cascade of damage similar to that of rattlesnake venom. The toxins tear apart red blood cells and platelets, leaving the victim vulnerable to brain hemorrhaging and uncontrolled bleeding. Clots form in the bloodstream, blocking the tiny blood vessels around the kidneys, the middle layer of the heart, and the brain. As the kidneys give out, the body swells with excess waste fluids. Complications ripple through all major organ systems, leading to strokes, blindness, epilepsy, paralysis, and heart failure. Though doctors can manage HUS symptoms, and are working on new ways to stymie the toxin, they currently can offer no cure or even effective treatment.

For public health officials, the emergence of *E. coli* O157:H7 is an object lesson in how a new pathogen can lie low in the environment, biding its time until humankind changes a certain activity and in so doing rolls out a red carpet. Like other emerging pathogens, such as the AIDS virus, O157 had struck long before it caught the attention of public health officials. In 1955, a Swiss pediatrician in a dairy farm area first described HUS, which physicians today consider to be a gauge of *E. coli* O157:H7 infection. Over the ensuing years, the number of cases kept rising, suggesting that O157 was quietly spreading. In 1975, doctors took a stool sample from a middle-aged California woman with bloody diarrhea, cultured the apparently rare bacterium and sent it to the CDC [Centers for Disease Control and Prevention], where it sat in storage until the McDonald's outbreak prompted researchers to scour their records for earlier evidence of the vicious organism. In other words, for nearly 30 years before the first bona fide epidemic, *E. coli* O157:H7 had turned up in scattered, sporadic cases of bloody diarrhea. It was out in the meat supply, but not in high enough concentrations to catch health officials' notice.

The Evolutionary History of O157:H7

Where did *E. coli* O157:H7 come from in the first place? Scientists have pieced together a long, rather provocative history. Genetic lineages suggest that about 50,000 years ago, O157 and another closely related serotype—O55:H7, which causes infant diarrhea in developing nations—split off from the same mother cell. Since then, O157 has taken part in a series of biological mergers and acquisitions that left it as vigorous as one of today's giant pharmaceutical houses. Indeed, a 2001 study showed that O157, composed of more than 5,400 genes, picks up foreign DNA at a much faster rate than do other organisms: At some point, it acquired two deadly Shiga toxin genes after being infected by a bacteriophage, a tiny virus that insinuates its DNA into the chromosome of a bacterium. In the microbial world, phages are like squatters . . . casually taking up residence in new bacteria, perhaps as a response to environmental stresses such as ultraviolet light or toxic chemicals. Bacteriophages are also the villains behind some of the most deadly human plagues; the genes coding for the cholera toxin, for instance, were borne on a phage. So what surrounding pressures compelled the phage carrying the Shiga toxin genes to light out for a new home in *E. coli?* In experiments on mice, Tufts University researcher David Acheson may have found the answer. When Acheson gave the animals low levels of antibiotics, the phage virus wildly replicated itself, and its magnified forces were more likely to infect other bacteria. Antibiotics also incited the phage to pour out clouds of Shiga toxin. Acheson speculates that when farmers began the practice of feeding cattle small doses of antibiotics to spur growth, beginning in the 1950s—perhaps not coincidentally, when the first reports of sporadic HUS in children came out—they may have unleashed O157. More backing for this theory comes from epidemiological evidence. *E. coli* O157:H7 is a disease of affluent, developed nations—which also happen to be the ones that feed growth-promoting antibiotics to livestock.

> **FAST FACT**
>
> According to a 2005 report in the *Journal of Food Production, E. coli* O157:H7 costs the United States $405 million per year—$370 million due to premature death of infected persons, $30 million for medical care, and $5 million in lost productivity.

Other Bacteria May Acquire Shiga Toxin

What worries Acheson and other scientists is that the restless phages that manufacture Shiga toxin may jump to other disease-causing bacteria. Actually, they've already proven they're disposed to do this, having set up home in about 200 other strains of *E. coli.* One of these, *E. coli* O111:H8, in 1999 caused a massive epidemic of nausea, vomiting, bloody diarrhea, and severe stomach cramps at a high school drill team camp in Texas, sickening dozens of the 750 teenage girls who attended. Though investigators never did find where the organism was hiding, they suspect it was either in the ice the girls used to soothe their parched throats during the drills or somewhere in the salad bar.

Shiga toxin phages have also landed in *Enterobacter* and *Citrobacter*—other bacteria that stir up intestinal disease. To find out just how prevalent these mysterious strains of dangerous *E. coli* may be, Acheson analyzed ground beef samples from 12 supermarkets in Boston and Cincinnati. The results came as a shock. He found Shiga toxin in a quarter of the samples—toxin produced not by O157:H7, but by other kinds of *E. coli*. And this may not be the end of their roving, Acheson warns. "Suppose something like *Salmonella* developed the ability to produce Shiga toxins. That could be an extremely deadly pathogen." Not only is *Salmonella* common, but, more than *E. coli* O157, it has a talent for quickly invading the bloodstream, meaning it could speedily convey Shiga toxins throughout the body like tiny poison-tipped missiles. Even more problematic, the antibiotics normally used to treat *E. coli* O157:H7 infections may actually aggravate the illness, by kicking phages into overdrive and stepping up their production of toxins, leading to hemolytic uremic syndrome.

New Ways of Fighting O157 Being Developed

Along its evolutionary path, *E. coli* also became acid resistant, so impervious to a low pH environment that it can survive the incredibly sour bath in the human stomach. Grain-feeding cattle, which supplanted traditional hay feeding after World War II, may have made the bacteria more acid resilient. Because of this acid tolerance, as few as 10 organisms are enough to cause infection. Having acquired a mean set of toxin genes, acid resistance, and other virulence properties, all *E. coli* O157:H7 needed to become a truly fearsome threat was access. That it acquired by spreading in domesticated cattle and then entering the gears of modern industrial meat production, all within the past 25 years. Unfortunately, O157 may have left the door open behind it. Other strains of *E. coli*, "if tweaked in the right way" by phages and the mobile rings of DNA known as plasmids, could negotiate the same path, says Tom Whittam, a biologist at Pennsylvania State University who has studied O157 evolution.

Research is under way on vaccines that would prevent cattle from carrying O157, and on feed additives—including competing intestinal bacteria—that would eliminate the pathogenic organism in livestock. Thoroughly cooking ground beef to a temperature of 160 degrees Fahrenheit is the proven method of killing *E. coli* O157:H7. But in the United States, the organism retains a fighting chance because of the American love affair with rare burgers, which practically guarantees that one man's meat will be another man's poison. As a restaurant menu in suburban Dallas proudly informs its customers: "The Department of Health suggests MEDIUM-WELL for any ground beef product. Our burgers are cooked MEDIUM (PINK) unless you request otherwise."

Finding the Source of Food-Borne Disease Outbreaks Is Difficult

Elizabeth Weise

Elizabeth Weise is a science reporter for *USA Today,* covering topics such as biotechnology, agriculture, and food safety. In the following viewpoint she explains the process whereby a food-borne disease outbreak is discovered and ultimately traced to the source, describing in detail a 2008 case of *Salmonella*-contaminated tomatoes. According to Weise, the complexity of modern food production and distribution system makes it challenging to uncover the cause of such a disease outbreak. Weise reports that a local health-care worker initially realized an outbreak was occurring. After state and federal agencies were notified, many detailed patient interviews were conducted, laboratory tests were done, and the data were analyzed until the ultimate source of the contamination was determined, culminating in the Food and Drug Administration issuing a national warning to the public.

The contamination of tomatoes with a rare strain of *Salmonella* has led to the largest outbreak of food-borne illnesses since E. coli in spinach killed five and sickened hundreds almost two years ago [in 2006].

At least 277 people of all ages in 28 states and the District of Columbia have been sickened; 43 have been hospitalized. A nationwide recall of round, plum and Roma tomatoes has dealt a sharp blow to the $2.7 billion fresh-tomato market, costing the food industry tens of millions of dollars.

But it could have been a lot worse if a red flag hadn't been raised early in the outbreak last month [May 2008] by a public health nurse with good instincts in one of the nation's poorest, most remote regions.

Indeed, health officials say that because the first cluster of patients surfaced on the Navajo Nation in New Mexico, where they are served by a small, close-knit medical community, federal investigators were able to quickly identify the contaminated foods and take steps to contain the outbreak the past two weeks.

The Investigation Begins

After being the first to recognize the signs of an emerging outbreak, the federal Indian Health Service staff played a key role in the search for the tainted food. "It was 21st-century molecular epidemiology and old-fashioned boot leather," says John Redd, the infectious disease branch chief with the Indian Health Service in Albuquerque. "You've got to get out from behind your desk and hit the road sometimes."

Kimberlae Houk has 24 years of experience in public health nursing in the Navajo Nation, the largest reservation in the USA, with lands extending into Arizona, Utah and New Mexico.

Her Shiprock Indian Health Services Unit provides medical care to more than 45,500 American Indians, mostly Navajo, in an area that covers 23 communities in

the three states. Homes can be extremely isolated, and many are without telephones.

Houk knew something was up on Monday, May 19, [2008,] when four people very sick with diarrhea, fever and abdominal cramps showed up at the Northern Navajo Medical Center in Shiprock, N.M.

"A lot of time with these kinds of diseases you get your babies and your grandmas in the hospital," she says. "But in this one we had fit 30-year-olds. And we just don't get 30-year-olds in the hospital with dehydration."

And these people weren't just dropping in at the doctor's office. "We serve a very rural population. They have to drive an hour to the clinic and an hour back. So it's a big deal to come in," Houk says.

A sign on a McDonald's restaurant informs customers that tomatoes have been pulled from its menu until the source of a *Salmonella* contamination has been found. (**Russel A. Daniels/AP Images**)

With previous experience with outbreaks of measles, whooping cough, hantavirus and even the plague, Houk immediately went into outbreak mode. "We literally drop everything when there's a communicable disease, to protect people."

That day, "We all just ran," says Houk. "We can really get on top of things quickly because all our nurses, our doctors, our clinics, our labs, we're all under the same roof."

State and Federal Health Departments Notified

Salmonella is a bacteria found in animal intestines that can be transmitted when foods are contaminated by animal feces. It's a reportable condition, meaning if it pops up anywhere, state and federal health departments must be notified.

Suspecting that bacteria could have sickened their patients, Houk and her colleagues sent stool samples to New Mexico's state laboratory. The tests showed that the patients had saintpaul—one of 2,300 different strains of *Salmonella,* and a very rare one.

Next the state lab did a genetic fingerprint on the bacteria to make sure that all were indeed the exact same strain.

"Our lab called us on May 21, which was a Wednesday," says Paul Ettestad, who works in the state's infectious disease epidemiology bureau. The *Salmonella* saintpaul cases all had the exact same DNA fingerprint. It was all one outbreak.

Over the next two days, cases appeared in several New Mexican counties. Some patients were Navajo, some were not. All were very ill. "That really starts ringing the bells," Ettestad says. He contacted Ian Williams, chief of

> **FAST FACT**
>
> The Centers for Disease Control and Prevention estimates that only about 3 percent of the estimated 1.4 million cases of *Salmonella* poisoning in the United States are officially reported each year.

the outbreak team at the Centers for Disease Control and Prevention [CDC].

Cases were starting to pop up in Texas, too. "We had two cases reported out of Houston on the 22nd, and an additional 12 on the 23rd. Things moved pretty quickly," says Linda Gaul, head of the food-borne illness team at the Texas Department of State Health Services.

Then New Mexico posted the genetic fingerprints of its cases onto PulseNet, the CDC's computer disease-tracking network. Within hours, matches began to show up. The outbreak wasn't just in New Mexico and Texas, it was all over the country.

Finding the Common Thread

Now came the challenge: What connected a patient on remote Navajo lands with the other patients throughout the nation?

Even though it was Memorial Day weekend, every-one mobilized to work. New Mexico, Texas, the CDC and the Indian Health Service began holding daily con-ference calls. As other states got patients, they joined in. New Mexico started the calls, but eventually CDC took over hosting them because they "can accommodate 100 people on their lines," Houk says.

In a case like this, epidemiologists, the doctors who study outbreaks, pull out what they call a "shotgun sur-vey." It's a long—in this case 22 pages—survey that cov-ers just about anything a person might eat, drink or be exposed to that could cause such an illness.

"'Shotgun,' because it's like shooting in the dark to see what's there," says Texas' Gaul.

Enter the Indian Health Service again, charged with the task of administering the survey in the Navajo Na-tion, which by sheer chance seemed to have gotten the most cases in New Mexico.

"Our Indian Health nurses would drive two or three hours to try to find these people and when they couldn't find them, they'd have to go back," he says.

Steps in a Food-Borne Disease Outbreak Investigation

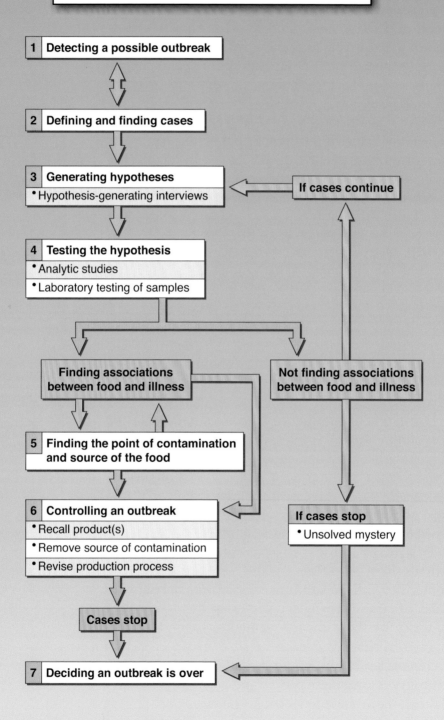

1 Detecting a possible outbreak

2 Defining and finding cases

3 Generating hypotheses
* Hypothesis-generating interviews

If cases continue

4 Testing the hypothesis
* Analytic studies
* Laboratory testing of samples

Finding associations between food and illness

Not finding associations between food and illness

5 Finding the point of contamination and source of the food

6 Controlling an outbreak
* Recall product(s)
* Remove source of contamination
* Revise production process

If cases stop
* Unsolved mystery

Cases stop

7 Deciding an outbreak is over

Taken from: Centers for Disease Control and Prevention.

Also, each nurse had to painstakingly reconstruct everything their patient had eaten in the previous two weeks. "Nurses pulled out calendars for clients and said, 'Where were you? Who were you with? What meal did you have with that event? What did you do before the event, and what did you eat later in the day?'" says Houk.

Not only that, but the surveys had to be given in three languages: English, Spanish and "English with Navajo clarification," Redd says.

"The folks in New Mexico really did an amazing job," says CDC's Williams. "Extraordinary."

Looking for Patterns in the Data

By Saturday more than a dozen of these questionnaires were completed. Epidemiologists and public health workers pored over them, looking for patterns. Jessica Jungk, a master of public health who also helped track spinach in the 2006 E. coli outbreak, got called in to help analyze the data. But while tomatoes were high on the list of foods eaten, they weren't a strong enough presence to be isolated as the problem.

Ettestad got on the phone with CDC's Williams, who urged really zeroing in on what people were eating. "Get them to open their refrigerators, their pantries" while they talk, he suggested.

To do that, a nurse was sent into a patient's home "and she literally pointed at every shelf on the refrigerator and every cabinet and asked, 'Did you eat anything on this shelf?' It's a difficult thing to do. It makes people feel anxious," Houk says.

But it did the trick. Even people who swear they didn't eat raw tomatoes remember they might have when asked about salsa or guacamole or a slice of tomato on a hamburger. On Saturday, with surveys coming in not only from New Mexico but a few other states as well, the percentage of patients who'd eaten fresh tomatoes stood at 75%, compared with an average of 68% of random Americans. By

Sunday, with more cases analyzed, the share shot up to 83%, Ettestad says.

But that wasn't enough to nail tomato as the culprit. Next came the scientific gold standard, a case control survey to look at whether people who didn't get sick ate significantly less of the suspect food than people who did. For this, the investigators employed a tried and true tool for random selection: spin-the-bottle.

The key to a good case control is randomness. Investigators want to compare healthy people with those who got sick, but they want them to be similar in every other way, and they don't want to bias who gets chosen. Today epidemiologists use computerized phone books and an Internet randomizing program.

But a lot of the people they needed to talk to didn't even have phones.

So they want back to the old techniques. "You go out to the house of someone who got sick. You take a bottle and put it on the ground. You spin it and you go in the direction it points until you hit a house," Ettestad says. "And that's just as random as the Internet."

Redd of the Indian Health Service didn't even have a bottle: "I was spinning a government-issue pen."

By Saturday, May 31, New Mexico was ready to start warning people. "We felt we had enough evidence and we needed to protect our citizens," Ettestad says.

Three days later FDA [Food and Drug Administration] issued a warning for Texas and New Mexico. Five days later, with cases appearing across the nation, FDA made the warning national.

The agency was able to quickly announce where the tomatoes didn't come from because most tomato-growing areas weren't harvesting in late April when the first cases showed up. It soon became clear that mid-Florida and Mexico were the only major growing areas selling tomatoes at that point.

The Investigation Continues

Efforts to pinpoint the source of the contaminated tomatoes are ongoing, and the FDA is still identifying clusters of cases and backtracking to the suppliers.

Food producers say the financial impact could surpass that of the spinach contamination. At least 50% of Americans eat tomatoes regularly, but only 4% eat spinach, according to the NPD Group, a market research firm.

Tomato sales have fallen amid reduced demand from grocers and restaurants, and prices for varieties affected by the outbreak have likewise dropped, says Mark Munger, vice president of marketing for Andrew & Williamson Fresh Produce.

Major restaurant chains such as McDonald's are once again using tomatoes, carefully sourced to make sure they came from regions that weren't implicated in the outbreak. They're also back in supermarkets, often with notes posted above them about where the tomatoes were picked and why those areas were safe.

But consumers will remain wary, especially if the FDA can't locate the source of the outbreak, says Tom Nassif, CEO of Western Growers, which represents growers in Arizona and California.

The outbreak is a reminder that consumers pay a price for the vast agricultural production and distribution system that supplies cheap, plentiful produce year round, says Kenneth Albala, a food historian at the University of the Pacific in Stockton, Calif.

"In the past most food was produced and consumed locally, you wouldn't have much trouble figuring out where (tainted) food came from," he says.

Today, he says, having fresh, ripe, cheap tomatoes available in salads nationwide in April—inconceivable two generations ago—also means "the distribution is so broad that something (contaminated) can show up in 13 states the next day."

CHAPTER 2

Controversies About Food-Borne Diseases

The Problem of Food-Borne Diseases Is Increasing

Madeline Drexler

Madeline Drexler is a journalist specializing in medicine, science, and public health. She is the editor of the *Harvard Public Health Review* and author of *Emerging Epidemics: The Menace of New Infections*. In the following viewpoint Drexler asserts that the distribution of food has become much more complex than in the past, with a corresponding increase in the complexity of food-borne disease outbreaks. She says that because of how widely food is distributed, the small-scale localized outbreaks of the past now have the potential to spread much farther and affect huge numbers of people. In addition, the author argues that many diseases that were formerly rare or completely unknown have become major problems. Drexler claims that there is much that is still unknown about food-borne diseases and how they may change in the future.

Photo on facing page. In an effort to reduce food-borne diseases, many people grow their own produce and sell it locally. (Lynn Ischay/The Plain Dealer/Landov)

SOURCE: Madeline Drexler, *Emerging Epidemics: The Menace of New Infections*. Washington, DC: Joseph Henry, 2010. Reprinted with permission from the National Academies Press, Copyright 2010, National Academy of Sciences.

One of the most insistent marketing messages we hear, trumpeted by both industry and regulators, is that the United States has the safest food supply in the world. Yet according to the CDC [Centers for Disease Control and Prevention]'s best calculations, each year 76 million Americans—nearly one in four, and that's a lowball estimate—become infected by what they eat. Most find themselves for a few days dolefully memorizing a pattern of bathroom floor tiles. About 325,000 land in the hospital. Two million suffer drawn-out, sometimes lifelong medical complications from unwittingly eating a contaminated morsel. More than 5,000— about 14 a day—die from indulging in what should be one of life's great pleasures. The "world's safest food supply" regularly doles out *E. coli* O157:H7 in hamburgers, *Salmonella* in alfalfa sprouts, *Listeria* in hot dogs, *Campylobacter* in Thanksgiving turkeys.

Change is what ushers new disease-causing organisms into our lives. And in the past few decades, there have been profound shifts in what we eat, where our food comes from, how it's made, and who makes it. Fifty years ago, grocery stores stocked about 200 items, 70 percent of which were grown, produced, or processed within a 100-mile radius of the store. Today, the average supermarket carries nearly 50,000 food items, some stores as many as 70,000. Agriculture and food manufacture have grown into global economies of scale, producing megaton quantities that, if contaminated, increase the potential for widespread epidemics. More fresh fruits and vegetables come from abroad, where sanitary standards may not be as high as in the United States. And our meals are increasingly cooked by people untrained in the techniques of safe food preparation.

Nature of Food Poisoning Has Changed

This is not your grandparents' "food poisoning"—a now-quaint term that originated early in the twentieth cen-

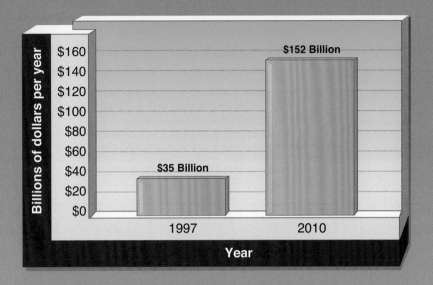

US Department of Agriculture Estimates of the High Cost of Food-Borne Diseases

$152 Billion

$35 Billion

Billions of dollars per year

$160
$140
$120
$100
$80
$60
$40
$20
$0

1997   2010

Year

Taken from: Andrew Zajac and P.J. Huffstutter, "Cost of Food-Borne Illnesses Is Deemed Much Higher than Earlier Estimates," *Los Angeles Times*, March 3, 2010.

tury, when dramatic gastrointestinal distress was usually traced to toxins, especially staph toxins, that had grown on spoiled foods such as cream-filled pastries or chicken salads left out too long in summer heat. Literally cases of food "intoxication," these infections struck suddenly and fiercely, usually within two to six hours after the meal. When local health officials worked up these classic "point source outbreaks," they would inevitably find that a knot of victims had all eaten a single dish, and that cases sharply climbed and then plummeted as the well of exposed individuals dried up. Point source outbreaks haven't faded away; big-city health departments face dozens every year. In 1997, for instance, *Salmonella*-tainted hams from a church fundraising dinner in St. Mary's County, Maryland, sickened 700 people and killed an elderly woman. Today, however, the modest church picnic has given way to a giant food bazaar created by massive consolidation and global distribution. One contaminated tidbit—a shred of meat from an infected steer mixed with hundreds of other carcasses for hamburger, an iced box of tainted lettuce dripping down on the rest of an outbound lot, a soiled production line of cereal shipped coast-to-coast under 30 different brand names—spreads disease far and wide.

Pathogens Have Changed, Too

The pathogens in science's crosshairs have also changed—in part because improved technology permits scientists to see some for the first time, and in part because evolution has selected for more noxious creatures. Twenty years ago, today's most fearsome threats were over-looked or yet-to-be-discovered. *Campylobacter jejuni*, now known to be the most common bacterial agent in food, was considered a rare, opportunistic organism because lab workers didn't see it hiding among less fastidious bacteria growing in culture. A small, delicate, spiral-shaped microbe, it corkscrews its way into mucous membranes of the intestinal tract "with a speed that cannot be matched by other bacteria," according to one scientist's report. *Listeria monocytogenes*, the most deadly agent in our food supply, killing one in five victims it infects, wasn't even suspected of spreading through food. *E. coli* O157:H7, a potent threat to children and the aged, was identified only in 1982—and even then remained a medical curiosity until the infamous 1993 Jack in the Box hamburger outbreak. Norwalk virus, the top cause of foodborne illness in this country at 23 million cases a year, remained largely elusive until molecular tests revealed it in the 1990s. All of which suggests there are novel disease-causing agents still hiding incognito in our food. Even with modern diagnostic tools, in 81 percent of foodborne illnesses and 64 percent of deaths, doctors don't know what organisms to blame—in part because they don't know what organisms to look for.

Food-Borne Diseases Have Become More Dangerous

To doctors and scientists, some of these bugs—particular *E. coli* O157:H7—are scarier than anything seen before. "Foodborne pathogens are not purely a bit of nausea and vomiting and diarrhea," says David Acheson, an *E. coli* researcher at Tufts University School of Medicine. "They can kill a previously healthy person in the space of a week." Evolutionary biologists fear that our efforts to eliminate pathogens on the farm and in processing—by, for example, using disinfectant rinses—may paradoxically help select for more durable and virulent strains.

Meanwhile, more of us are more vulnerable to foodborne microbes. Individuals with impaired immunity—the very young, the very old, and people with cancer, organ transplants, diabetes, AIDS, and other conditions that weaken the body's defenses; all told, about a quarter of the population—are more apt to succumb to these infections. Men and women over 65, who in the next three decades will make up one-fifth of the population, produce less acid in their stomachs, eliminating the first line of defense against enteric pathogens; federal officials predict that the aging population could increase foodborne illness by 10 percent in the next decade. Americans are popping more prescription and over-the-counter antacids than ever, and in so doing, giving pathogens entré to the nether regions of our digestive system where they do the most damage.

Depending on the organism, the palette of symptoms associated with foodborne disease can include diarrhea, cramps, fever, nausea, and vomiting (the notable exception is *Listeria*, which can cause miscarriage, meningitis,

FAST FACT

USA Today reports that cases of an infection by *Listeria monocytogenes,* a rare but deadly bacterial infection that causes 20 percent of deaths from food-borne diseases in the United States, increased by 22 percent in 2009.

and other nonabdominal problems). But that's just the beginning. In some people, researchers have discovered, the gastrointestinal distress that comes and goes with a foul meal may hang around in another form much longer. *Salmonella* can trigger reactive arthritis, an acute joint inflammation. *Campylobacter jejuni* may cause as many as 40 percent of cases of Guillain-Barré syndrome, a severe neurological disorder that can bring temporary paralysis and long-term nerve damage. Other complications include thyroid disease, inflammatory bowel disease, and, should someone survive the struggle against *E. coli* O157:H7, permanent kidney damage from hemolytic uremic syndrome. In these cases, contaminated food seems to provoke an uncontrolled autoimmune reaction. Up to 3 percent of foodborne disease victims—an enormous number, given the total caseload—may suffer lifelong physical problems.

Much Remains Unknown

Any depiction of emerging foodborne infections is necessarily panoramic, complex, and accompanied by more questions than answers. This discussion is no exception. . . . Debates about questions of farm management, government regulation, and individual versus institutional responsibility may elicit two—or three or four—diametrically opposed arguments that all seem persuasive. "Foodborne illness is more complex than people understand. The more I learn, the less I realize I ever knew," says Mike Osterholm, a former Minnesota state epidemiologist who has probably launched more successful food outbreak investigations than any other public health official in history. "The very nature of the ever-growing and complex food supply chain, and the desire of consumers to have many different kinds of foods available at a moment's notice, has allowed for a whole new spectrum of pathogens to arrive on the scene." What's more, says Osterholm, DNA fin-

gerprinting has pulled back the covers from foodborne outbreaks, showing that "many of the old conclusions we had drawn about what was happening are not valid."

For those of us who don't think about it for a living, it's easy to underestimate the risk of falling ill from food, since the problem is largely invisible—hidden, one supposes, behind the bathroom door. CDC epidemiologists have factored in this cultural aversion by using numerical multipliers that translate the relatively few cases reported into a far higher and more accurate count of victims who never see a doctor. For instance, for every person known to suffer an infection caused by *Campylobacter* or *Salmonella* or *Cyclospora*, there are 38 who have eluded the net of public health officials; for every confirmed case of *E. coli* O157:H7, there are 13 to 27 doubled-over victims. Keep this in mind when you read news stories about foodborne epidemics. The scores of confirmed cases mentioned in wire service stories may actually represent hundreds or thousands of silent sufferers.

Because food distribution has become so complex, companies such as Armstrong Produce began to use radio tracking to trace produce from farm to market in order to improve food safety. (Ronen Zilberman/AP Images)

Foodborne infections are ubiquitous, sneaky, and regularly sold short. At the CDC, the foodborne and diarrheal diseases branch investigates more outbreaks than any other group in the agency. According to Paul Mead, a medical epidemiologist, "The paradox of foodborne illness is that, on a per meal basis, it's extremely rare. It's like getting hit by a meteor." But in the very act of eating, says Mead, "You're standing in a meteor shower three times a day from the time you're weaned until you die."

Food-Borne Disease Scares Are Exaggerated

T.J. Greaney

T.J. Greaney is a reporter with the *Columbia Daily Tribune,* a newspaper based in Columbia, Missouri. In the following viewpoint Greaney argues that the fear people have of food-borne diseases is greatly exaggerated. He points out that public announcements of unsafe food are often so vague as to be meaningless, offering as an example an announcement from the Centers for Disease Control and Prevention in 2008 warning people to avoid "raw, red, round-shaped tomatoes." Greaney also recounts several examples of what he considers to be overblown food scares from his childhood. He dismisses suggestions that food supplies need to be more traceable, arguing instead that what is needed is a greater diversity of more localized food sources. According to the author, this would reduce the tendency for food-borne diseases to affect large numbers of people.

SOURCE: T.J. Greaney, Against the Grain Column: "It Just Is Not Summer Without a Food Scare," *Columbia Daily Tribune,* June 19, 2008. Reproduced by permission.

I pulled up to the drive-through at a local sub shop recently and saw a sign taped to the menu: "Due to recommendations by the FDA [Food and Drug Administration], we are not currently offering tomatoes in any of our sandwiches. We apologize for the inconvenience."

I immediately knew what I was dealing with. It wouldn't be summer without a food scare on the national level. Greatest hits from years past have included tainted chicken pot pies, *E. coli* in the green onions at Taco Bell and surprise cans of spinach. These scares pop up, inspire a few jokes for late-night comedians, fill time on cable news and quickly disappear.

Reports of Dangerous Food Are Too Vague

Later that day, I heard the gory details in a radio report. The announcer said the Centers for Disease Control and Prevention had confirmed more than 100 cases of food poisoning from *Salmonella* bacteria across several states. People as far apart as New Mexico and New Jersey were reporting abdominal discomfort, fever and diarrhea after eating the red fruit.

Officials warned it was best to avoid "raw, red, round-shaped tomatoes" that "do not have the vine still attached."

If the FDA had been a police sketch artist drawing up a "wanted" poster for this fugitive tomato, they had produced the worst one ever.

It described every tomato I've ever laid eyes on. In fact, I thought as my veins chilled just a bit, I ate a round, vine-less tomato just the day before. And my abdomen, well, it did feel just a tad cramped. Welcome to "Tomato Scare 2008." Gentlemen, man your battle stations.

Food Hysteria Starts in Grade School

Luckily, I'm a veteran of all types of food hysteria. In grade school, I remember coming home after eating a delicious burger from Jack in the Box. My friend Andy was horrified. "You ate at What's in the Box?" he exclaimed. "Kids have been dying from eating their burgers." My face turned green. "It's probably not too late to stick your finger down your throat," he added helpfully.

I survived that one.

Some years later, in high school, I was just about to dig into a Dairy Queen Heath Bar Blizzard when my sister piped up: "A boy in my class went into anaphylactic shock after he ate one of those. He's still in a coma."

I took my chances.

During my senior year of college, one of my housemates swore off beef. He said he'd been scared by all the news reports of cows twitching around in their pens before falling over.

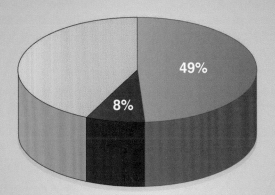

Food Recalls Seriously Impact Consumer Confidence

49%

8%

■ Percentage of consumers less likely to buy food product after it is recalled
■ Percentage saying they would not buy that product ever again

Taken from: "Less than 20% of Consumers Trust Food They Buy Is Safe and Healthy, IBM Reveals" (IBM Press Release), June 24, 2009.

"It can stay dormant in your body for 30 years or more," he told me as he self-righteously fried up one of the veggie burgers he had begun storing in the freezer. "Just watch—a bunch of cases are going to start turning up. It might take years for people to start showing the symptoms, but people already have it."

So this tomato deal hadn't thrown me for much of a loop. I'm a battle-scarred veteran.

A Greater Diversity of Food Would Reduce Risk

In fact, I find food scares fascinating. How is it that a nation of 300 million can all be asked to avoid eating the same thing? Are our food sources that inbred? Are we all eating from the same trough?

Yesterday [June 18, 2008], in the *Chicago Tribune*, a reporter interviewed David Acheson, the "food safety czar" at the Food and Drug Administration. He said the FDA has mainly been using a "process of elimination" to narrow down the possible sources of the *Salmonella* tomatoes based on growing seasons and map locations of people who have fallen ill.

Acheson said vegetables might need some equivalent to the Universal Product Code found on sealed packaging in the supermarket. There needs to be a greater degree of "traceability," he said.

Here's an idea Acheson will never ask for: How about a little more diversity? If chain restaurants and chain markets could be persuaded to buy more of their goods from local sources, we wouldn't have these scares every year. Additionally, regional vegetables have small genetic differences that make it less likely that a disease can jeopardize an entire food source at once. The bacteria that live in California tomatoes might not stand as much of a chance with their Missouri cousins.

> **FAST FACT**
>
> According to the Centers for Disease Control and Prevention, an estimated 5,000 people die of food-borne diseases in the United States each year; in comparison, over 50,000 deaths result from influenza and pneumonia, and over 120,000 from accidents.

In 2008 Dr. David Acheson, the "food safety czar" for the Food and Drug Administration, reported that the agency used a "process of elimination" to narrow down the possible sources of *Salmonella*-contaminated tomatoes. (**Susan Walsh/AP Images**)

It's why the word ["locavore"] has become such a catch phrase recently. People are rebelling against foods that are more homogenous and less hearty than ever before. If I'm going to ingest a food-borne illness, they say, at least let it be one of my own, locally grown food-borne illnesses. Don't outsource that job.

Today, the tomato scare appears to be on the wane. Although two cases of *Salmonella* were reported in eastern Missouri and linked to the current outbreak, Missouri-grown tomatoes were listed as safe to eat this week. Most local restaurants have returned them to the menus.

But the hysteria never goes away for long. Next time I see a sign posted on a menu, it might be lettuce or shrimp or tofu. It's all part of the same sad charade that stokes hysteria and never seems to make our food any safer.

The Federal Government Is Failing to Protect the Public Against Food-Borne Diseases

Andrew Kimbrell

Andrew Kimbrell is a writer, environmental attorney, and executive director of the Center for Food Safety. He is the author of *Your Right to Know: Genetic Engineering and the Secret Changes in Your Food,* and general editor of *Fatal Harvest: The Tragedy of Industrial Agriculture.* In the following viewpoint Kimbrell argues that the risk of food-borne disease in America is increasing due to cuts in funding for the agencies that regulate food, as well as a confusing array of regulations and responsible agencies. He also claims that existing federal regulations place an unfair burden on small and family farms, which he says have not been contributors to large food-borne disease outbreaks. Kimbrell recommends that a unified Food Safety Agency be created that will regulate the food industry in a more consistent fashion.

SOURCE: Andrew Kimbrell, "Food Safety in the US: We're on Red Alert," www.huffingtonpost.com, April 12, 2010. Reproduced by permission of the author.

The United States once had one of the safest food systems in the world, but now, 70 million Americans are sickened, 300,000 are hospitalized, and 5,000 die from food-borne illness every year. It is a sad fact: since 9/11, far more Americans have been killed, injured or hurt because of our lack of a coordinated food safety system than by terrorist acts that challenge our Homeland Security system.

The culprits in this assault on American well-being aren't shadowy terrorist figures, but rather, they are what most consumers would identify as wholesome—not harmful—foods. Peanuts, lettuce, pistachios, spinach, hamburgers sold to Boy Scout camps, peppers, tomatoes, and pepper-coated sausages are among the foods that have sickened and killed Americans in just the last few years. Our children are most at risk from these food threats, with half of all food-borne illness striking children under 15 years old.

Most Food Facilities Are Not Inspected

The [George W.] Bush administration constantly claimed it was protecting Americans from potential security threats, yet it completely failed to protect the public from the clear and present danger of deadly food. Due in part to that administration's cuts in funding and staff, the Food and Drug Administration (FDA) currently inspects less than 25% of all food facilities in the U.S. More than 50% of all American food facilities have gone uninspected for five years or more. During President Bush's last term, regulatory actions against those companies selling contaminated food to Americans declined by over a half.

The result is tragically predictable. Large processing facilities, which now mix foods from across the country and the world, are not being inspected. Illnesses caused by contaminated foods, which could be prevented with

Due to the George W. Bush administration's cuts in the FDA's funding and staff, the agency is able to inspect less than 25 percent of all food facilities in the United States. More than half of such facilities have gone uninspected for more than five years. (David R. Frazier/Photo Researchers, Inc.)

proper government oversight, are instead causing the hospitalization of hundreds of thousands and the deaths of thousands of Americans. Again, the victims are, disproportionately, our children.

The tens of millions of victims of food-borne illness represent only one segment of the casualties from our failure to require safe and nutritious food. Because of lax regulation of agricultural chemicals, many of the fruits and vegetables that should bring us health and nutrition are instead laced with dangerous pesticides, dozens of which are known carcinogens. Much of the food marketed to our children and served in their schools are confections brimming with trans-fats and high-fructose corn syrup; these contribute mightily to the epidemic of obesity in the young and heart disease and diabetes in our older populations. Under pressure from agribusiness, our federal agencies and legislators continue to commercialize genetically modified foods with no safety testing and no labeling for consumers. And, despite the strong potential of health hazards, food made with new, nanotechnology-based chemicals are getting waved through to the market, without any independent testing at all.

America's Food Safety System Is Broken

Clearly our food safety system is broken and needs a complete overhaul. With the continuing string of food contamination scandals, even Congress has begun to pay attention. The Food Safety Enhancement Act (HR 2749) was passed by the House of Representatives in the summer of

Annual Health-Related Costs from Food-Borne Diseases: Top Ten States

State	Billions of Dollars
California	$18.6
Texas	$11.3
New York	$10.4
Florida	$9.8
Pennsylvania	$6.7
Illinois	$6.5
Ohio	$5.8
Michigan	$5.0
Georgia	$4.7
New Jersey	$4.6

Taken from: Robert L. Scharff, "Health-Related Costs from Food-Borne Illness in the United States," Produce Safety Project at Georgetown University. www.producesafetyproject.org.

2008 and takes some steps in the right direction. It gives more authority to the FDA, restoring some of its power to conduct food inspections and strengthen oversight.

However, it's far from perfect. Bowing to pressure from agribusiness, lawmakers have exempted livestock producers and any other entity regulated by the USDA [United States Department of Agriculture] from the new regulations of both this act and its Senate companion, the Food Safety Modernization Act (S.510). In fact, members of Congress were so committed to the interests of big industrial meat producers that they also prohibited the FDA from "impeding, minimizing, or affecting" USDA authority on meat, poultry, and eggs. As a result, these bills contain the stupefying provision that no attempt by the FDA to combat *E. coli* and *Salmonella* will be allowed. These bacteria are the most common causes of deadly food-borne illness and are found in products contaminated with animal feces. Since January 2010, over 850,000 pounds of beef—mostly from industrial feed lots—has been recalled due to *E. coli* O157:H7 contamination. The members of Congress have essentially protected the interests of corporations who are bad actors, while condemning the public to continued sickness from these contaminants.

FAST FACT

According to the Government Accountability Office, the US Department of Agriculture regulates 20 percent of the food supply but has twice the budget of the Food and Drug Administration, which regulates the remaining 80 percent.

Another major problem with both bills is that they begin with the flawed premise that all producers and processors of food—whether massive corporate farms or small family farms—are equally at fault for our broken food safety system. New food safety legislation should target the largest causes of food-borne illness. These include concentrated animal feeding operations (CAFOs), water and field contamination due to manure lagoon leakage, and industrial processing systems, not small farms.

A New Food Safety System Is Needed

The "one size fits all" regulatory approach in these bills fails to take this disparity into account. It instead places an undue and unsupportable burden on family farms, small processors, and direct marketers of organic and locally grown food. These have not been contributors to the contamination events which have caused major food-borne illness outbreaks. Further support for this view is that, at a July 2009 House Oversight Subcommittee on Domestic Policy hearing on Ready-to-Eat Vegetables and Leafy Green Agreements, then-Senior FDA Adviser Michael R. Taylor acknowledged that "since 1999 outbreaks of food-borne pathogens were traced to leafy greens involved in precut packaged leafy greens and not whole leafy greens."

It is unconscionable that factory farms would get a pass under the proposed legislation while family farmers, who often struggle to stay in operation, are held to stringent, unnecessary and potentially bankrupting requirements. Small operators would bear the brunt of large fees that generate the revenue sufficient for the overall food safety program to operate. Food safety regulation at the farm and processing level must be appropriate to scale and level of risk.

Fortunately, some Senators are addressing the gaps in their bill. Perhaps the most critical action so far is that of Sen. [Jon] Tester (D-MT), who has introduced an amendment to exempt small-scale and direct marketing farmers and processors, who are already well regulated by local authorities.

However, most problematic is that the legislation in its current state perpetuates the regulatory tangle that is our food safety system. Arcane mixes of regulatory authority between the FDA, USDA and EPA [Environmental Protection Agency] make for dangerously inefficient government. It is long overdue that we establish a separate and effective government agency dedicated to food safety. We need to separate out the "Food" part of the Food and Drug Administration and consolidate all authority under a new Food Safety Agency.

We did this for Homeland Security; we should also do it for food security. After all, it is the lack of food safety in this country that is the far more imminent threat to all of us, our families and, especially, our children.

The National School Lunch Program Is Susceptible to Food-Borne Diseases

Michael Markarian

Michael Markarian is executive vice president of the Humane Society of the United States and president of the Fund for Animals. He is also president of the Humane Society Legislative Fund and writes the *Animals & Politics* blog for that organization. In the following viewpoint Markarian discusses a report from the US Department of Agriculture's Office of the Inspector General, which uncovered cases of sick cattle being treated inhumanely as well as shortcomings in the meat inspection system that could result in safety issues being overlooked. The focus of the investigation, according to Markarian, is on "cull" cattle plants that deal with weak and physically depleted cows. He says that much of the meat that goes to supply school lunch programs comes from facilities that were investigated in the report. Markarian cites scientific reports that found a high degree of contamination by *E. coli* O157:H7 and *Salmonella*—both serious sources of food-borne diseases—in cull cattle plants, and says the fact that so much meat for schools is coming from these plants is a serious problem.

SOURCE: Michael Markarian, "Serving Sickness to School Kids," www.huffingtonpost.com, December 15, 2008. Reproduced by permission of the author.

Last week [early December 2008], the U.S. Department of Agriculture [USDA]'s Office of the Inspector General [OIG] released its long-awaited audit of slaughter practices and procedures, launched after The Humane Society of the United States uncovered rampant cruelty to sick and crippled cows at the Hallmark/Westland meat packing plant in Chino, Calif., earlier this year.

The report inexplicably claims that the abuses which led to the largest meat recall in U.S. history are not "systemic" in the industry, but then goes on to explain numerous ways that similar problems could be occurring at other plants. At a time when agribusiness operations knew they were under heightened scrutiny and were arguably on their best behavior, the investigation still found dangerous gaps in the system. As Neil Nisperos reported in the [California newspapers the] *Inland Valley Daily Bulletin* and *San Bernardino County Sun*: The OIG concluded there was an "inherent vulnerability" for handling violations to occur and not be detected by USDA inspectors because the agency does not provide continuous surveillance of all areas in a slaughter establishment.

The investigation also found several veterinarians who took shortcuts in ante-mortem [before death] inspections in order to complete assigned tasks. Such shortcomings made it possible for problems to be missed.

FAST FACT

The Centers for Disease Control and Prevention reports that about half of documented food-borne diseases occur in children, a majority of whom are under fifteen years old.

Abused Animals and Unsafe Food

It's clear that lax agency enforcement of humane slaughter rules continues to allow unacceptable abuse of animals and food safety risks. It's an issue to which the incoming [Barak] Obama administration and the new Congress must be attentive, as we urgently need stronger oversight and reform to prevent inhumane treatment of

Steve Mendell (pictured), head of the Hallmark/Westland meat-packing plant in Chino, California, testifies before a congressional committee regarding the company's inhumane practices in the slaughter of cattle. **(Chuck Kennedy/MCT/ Landov)**

animals, reduce the risks of foodborne illness and boost consumer confidence in the food supply.

The OIG audit focused on "cull cattle" plants which, like Hallmark/Westland, specialize in slaughtering "spent" dairy cows—those who have been pushed to their limits of milk production and are generally in weaker physical condition than other cows. One of the most shocking revelations in the new report is that four of the facilities investigated supply meat to processors who provide nearly 60 percent of all ground beef to the National School Lunch Program.

When the public first saw images of crippled cows being abused with bulldozers, electric prods, and water hoses, people were horrified to learn that meat from this one particular plant—which had been named the USDA "supplier of the year" for the 2004–2005 academic year—was being served to thousands of school children in 47 states. Now we know that an overwhelming amount of ground beef in school lunches still comes from cull cattle plants—where cows are more likely to be too weak and sick to stand up and walk on their own.

Dangerously Contaminated Meat

A review of new scientific studies reveals just how dangerous this current practice is not only for animals but also for school children. In the August 2008 issue of the *Journal of Food Protection*, USDA researchers report that after analyzing more than 1,000 beef samples, half from cull cattle slaughter plants and half from regular plants, they found more than three times the presence of *Salmonella* in the cull cattle meat. Also, all of the multidrug-resistant *Salmonella* they found came from cull cattle.

In October 2008, a different set of USDA researchers sampled carcasses at cull cattle slaughter plants across the country and found an astounding 94.3 percent of cull cattle hides contaminated with either *E. coli* O157:H7, *Salmonella*, or both. They then documented the transfer of these pathogens from the hides to the carcasses through to the end of the process. The potentially deadly strain of *E. coli* O157:H7 is the leading cause of acute kidney failure among school children in North America, and *Salmonella* is another leading foodborne killer.

Our schools have become a dumping ground for cheap meat, and it's coming from the very slaughter plants where the animals are more likely to be sick and injured, and the meat is more likely to be contaminated. The most

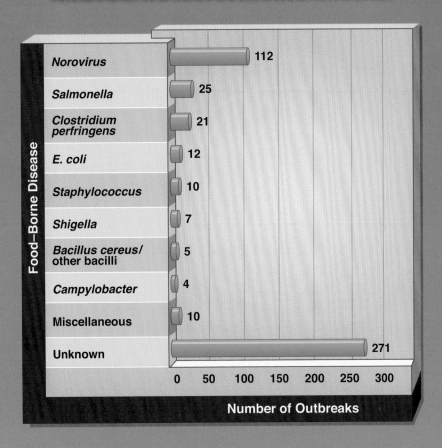

Food-Borne Disease Outbreaks in Schools, 1998–2007

Food-Borne Disease	Number of Outbreaks
Norovirus	112
Salmonella	25
Clostridium perfringens	21
E. coli	12
Staphylococcus	10
Shigella	7
Bacillus cereus/other bacilli	5
Campylobacter	4
Miscellaneous	10
Unknown	271

Taken from: *USA Today* analysis of data from the Centers for Disease Control and Prevention.

vulnerable populations of our society are subjected to the lowest-grade food with the highest-grade risk.

It's a disgrace that nearly a year has passed since the Hallmark/Westland scandal, with agencies and businesses not doing much differently when it comes to school lunches or slaughter practices. Lawmakers and federal regulators need to do better for farm animals and for children, and usher in a whole new era of oversight and reform for food safety and humane treatment.

Food Irradiation Is Safe and Effective

Ron Eustice

Ron Eustice is executive director of the Minnesota Beef Council as well as Minnesota's state coordinator for the Beef Quality and Safety Assurance Program. In the following viewpoint Eustice argues that food irradiation is a vital tool that can vastly increase the food supply to feed a hungry and growing world population. He says that irradiation has proven to be a safe technology and that Americans are already eating an increasing amount of irradiated food. According to Eustice, irradiation makes food much safer by destroying microorganisms that cause food-borne diseases.

The global population is projected to exceed 9 billion people by 2050, up from the 6.76 billion people on Earth today [in 2009]. Thanks to continuous improvements in animal husbandry and environmental stewardship and to modern technology,

SOURCE: Ron Eustice, "Tool Needed in World of Plenty: Irradiation Not Only Can Make Food Safer but Can Delay Spoilage, Increasing Food Supplies for People Around the World," *Feedstuffs*, vol. 30, 2009, p. 9. Reproduced by permission.

farmers and ranchers are producing more food now than at any other time in history.

During the 1960s and '70s, the "Green Revolution" used science and technology to increase yields and helped make many countries in the developing world self-sufficient in food production.

Hybrid seeds, chemical fertilizers, pesticides and irrigation produced yields previously considered impossible. Genetically improved livestock provided increasingly more meat and milk to meet human requirements for protein, calcium, iron and zinc.

Although the Green Revolution still needs to be completed in certain regions of the world, especially in sub-Saharan Africa, significant progress has been made.

Despite record-large food production, a recent U.N. report estimated that more than 1 billion people are considered hungry, consuming fewer than 1,800 calories per day. Why are so many people hungry in a world of plenty?

We must not oversimplify a complex situation driven by global economic weakness, civil and political instability, drought and unreliable distribution systems that have made food less affordable and accessible for a sizeable portion of the world's population. Although many of these problems are mostly beyond our control, we do have resources that can help improve the situation.

Irradiation Is a Serious Tool

Just as the Green Revolution used science and technology to feed a hungry world 50 years ago, it is imperative that we again turn to technology to prevent a global food crisis.

It is time to take a serious look at food irradiation as a tool that can help us alleviate hunger. Irradiation, which uses electronic energy, is a cost-effective and environmentally friendly technology that has the potential to do more to prevent food spoilage and alleviate hunger than any other technology currently available.

Irradiated beef hamburgers are served for lunch to several members of the US Department of Agriculture and the meat-processing industry at a Nebraska beef safety meeting in 1998. (S.E. McKee/AP Images)

Food losses and waste in the U.S. are as high as 50%, according to some recent estimates. As much as 25% of all fresh fruits and vegetables in the U.S. are lost between the field and the table. More than 50% of the food produced in the world is lost, wasted or discarded as a result of inefficiency in the human-managed food chain.

In Australia, it is estimated that food waste makes up half of the country's landfill. Almost one-third of all food purchased in the U.K. [United Kingdom] every year never gets eaten.

Losses between harvest and market in developing parts of the world can be as high as 40% of the harvest due to pathogens and pests.

Irradiation destroys harmful bacteria, prevents infestation of pests and, by doing so, can open markets where countries haven't previously been willing to import certain food items due to phytosanitary [clean and healthy plant foods] concerns. It also extends shelf life.

Irradiation is becoming more widely used around the world every day.

Although irradiated fruits, vegetables and poultry have been available commercially on a limited basis since the early 1990s, the introduction of irradiated ground beef in Minnesota in May 2000 significantly increased awareness and interest in the technology.

It's estimated that approximately 15 million to 18 million lb. of irradiated ground beef and poultry were consumed in the U.S. last year [2008]. An estimated 17 million lb. of irradiated fresh fruit and 10 million lb. of irradiated fresh produce were consumed in the U.S. in 2006.

It's estimated that one-third of commercial spices consumed in the U.S.—approximately 175 million lb.—are irradiated.

FAST FACT

According to the Centers for Disease Control and Prevention, irradiating 50 percent of the poultry and meat eaten in the United States would result in nine-hundred thousand fewer deaths from food-borne diseases each year.

Irradiation Destroys Harmful Bacteria

Although irradiation is being used to protect public health by eliminating harmful bacteria, there is a growing need to use irradiation to prevent food spoilage by extending the shelf life of meat, fruit, vegetables and other foods.

When food spoils and is thrown in the garbage, the cost is much more than the price of the food. We must also calculate the cost to produce the food and transport it to market. This cost includes the price of land on which the crop is grown, seed, fertilizer, labor, petroleum, water to irrigate the field, harvesting and transport. With 30–50% of the food we produce being wasted, the time has come to find a real solution to a very real problem.

Potential Annual Public Health Benefits of Irradiating 50 Percent of Meat and Poultry, by Specific Pathogen

Pathogen	Prevented cases	Prevented hospitalization	Prevented major complications	Prevented deaths
E. coli O157:H7	23,000	700	250 cases	20
Campylobacter	500,000	2,600	250 cases	25
Salmonella	330,000	4,000	6,000 cases	140
Listeria	625	575	60 miscarriages	125
Toxoplasma	28,000	625	100–1,000 cases	94
Total	881,625	8,500	6,660 illnesses	352

Taken from: www.choicesmagazine.org/2003-3/2003-3-06.htm.

Efforts to decrease global hunger and prevent a worldwide food crisis must take a multi-pronged approach, and routine adoption of food irradiation must be an essential component of that approach.

Irradiation is a powerful tool to help protect public health by eliminating harmful bacteria in meat, poultry and other foods produced and can save millions of pounds of valuable food by slowing spoilage and extending the shelf life of fresh and processed foods.

To expand the Green Revolution to regions of the world most affected by famine such as sub-Saharan Africa, farmers need several tools to grow crops and livestock, a processing and distribution infrastructure, modern retailing and ways to keep food safe and stable. Irradiation should be one of those tools.

At a news conference July 16, [2009,] Sen. Charles Grassley (Republican, Iowa), in response to a question about any specific recommendation he might offer for food safety legislation that would expand the authority of the Food and Drug Administration, said: "If they really want to take care of food safety, there ought to be promotion of irradiation."

Irradiation is a processing technology that eliminates harmful pathogens that can cause foodborne illnesses from foods such as ground beef, fruits, vegetables and spices. . . . Americans are increasingly consuming irradiated foods, including papaya and sweet potatoes from Hawaii, mangoes from India, guavas from Mexico and dragon fruit from Vietnam.

It is a food safety technology that's becoming more accepted. It's also a technology that delays spoilage, which means irradiated foods can be brought to markets from more distant producers and kept in refrigerators longer than usual. This decreases waste, and in reducing the amount of food that's thrown out, it's environmentally sustainable.

These features mean irradiation is not only a food safety intervention but stretches the food supply, giving it the expanded role of a tool for food production in parts of the world with undeveloped or underdeveloped infrastructures and for providing food where people are hungry.

Irradiation is something that at least one U.S. senator thinks should be promoted, irradiation is something consumers already get their teeth into and irradiation is something that creates a larger and safer food supply and more sustainable environment.

Food Irradiation Is Harmful

Organic Connections

Organic Connections is a natural foods magazine published by Peter Gillham's Natural Vitality, a company that sells nutritional supplements. In the following selection the author argues that food irradiation—the practice of using radiation to destroy pests and bacteria in food—is being used as an alternative to addressing basic sanitation issues in the food industry. Furthermore, the claim is made that not only has food irradiation not been proven safe, but there are reasons to suspect that it may cause harm. For example, irradiation produces "unique radiolytic products," new chemicals that are not normally present in food. The author also refers to studies showing that much of the vitamin content of food is destroyed by irradiation, noting that some dangerous disease–causing microorganisms, such as the bacterium that causes botulism, are resistant to radiation and therefore may thrive if competing microorganisms are killed off. The author suggests that instead of relying on radiation to sterilize food before it reaches the consumer, the root causes of unsafe food need to be comprehensively addressed first.

SOURCE: "Food Irradiation for Food Safety?" *Organic Connections,* May 2010. Reproduced by permission.

If you've seen the film *Food, Inc.*, you know that our industrial food system can be severely unsanitary. With the cramped conditions in which animals are bred, raised and slaughtered, it is no wonder that diseases such as *E. coli* spread so easily and end up in supermarkets and fast-food outlets. Because cattle ranches supply fertilizer to produce farms, such diseases can be spread to our fruits and vegetables as well.

Instead of solving the basic problems of sanitation in the food industry, a recent solution put into effect by food producers to prevent the spread of such bacteria is to irradiate food. According to research conducted by the Center for Food Safety (CFS), food irradiation uses high-energy gamma rays, electron beams or X-rays—all of which are millions of times more powerful than standard medical X-rays—to break apart the bacteria and insects that can hide in meat, grains and other foods.

The Center for Food Safety is a non-profit public interest and environmental advocacy membership organization with the purpose of challenging harmful food production technologies and promoting sustainable alternatives. Food irradiation has loomed large on their radar screen of late.

"There are a number of alarming facts about food irradiation," Bill Freese, Science Policy Analyst with CFS, told *Organic Connections*. "One thing is that it is an extremely high energy process that does a lot of undefined things to food components. In some cases it creates unique compounds that are not found anywhere else; they're called 'unique radiolytic products' (URPs). The science is still not there as to whether these compounds are hazardous to health or not, but there are a number of studies that suggest they are. These types of compounds are found especially in meats with higher fat

FAST FACT

The Center for Food Safety reports that food irradiation produces "unique radiolytic products"—chemicals that are produced only by irradiating food, including some substances that cause genetic mutations.

content. Some studies suggest that the process changes the fat molecules into compounds that, in the presence of carcinogenic compounds, intensify the carcinogens' impact. It kind of promotes the adverse impact of another known toxic compound."

According to data on the CFS website, irradiation also causes foods to lose from 2 to 95 percent of their vitamins. For example, irradiation can destroy up to 80 percent of the vitamin A in eggs, up to 95 percent of the vitamin A in green beans, up to 50 percent of the vitamin A in broccoli, and 40 percent of the beta carotene in orange juice. Irradiation also doubles the amount of trans fats in beef.

Freese cited other examples of nutrient reduction. "Vitamin C levels in spinach are very strongly reduced when it is irradiated, even at much lower than the maximum dose permitted by the FDA [Food and Drug Administration]. The B vitamin folate [which occurs naturally in food—folic acid is the synthetic form of folate found in supplements] is also reduced by significant amounts, and of course we all know folate is extremely important, especially for pregnant women, and is absolutely essential for developing embryos."

Irradiation and Botulism Risk

In addition to the killing of disease-causing microorganisms, another argument in favor of food irradiation is that it reduces spoilage and increases shelf life. Spoilage is reduced because microbes of all sorts are diminished, according to data from the Centers for Disease Control [and Prevention] website.

But in addition to the nutrients being killed off along with everything else, Freese explained another potential danger. "There are certain disease-causing microorganisms that are radiation resistant. One of them is the bacterium that causes botulism. Scientists have expressed concern that if you zap the spoilage microorganisms, which are more sensitive, then you create a clear playing

field for this kind of dangerous botulism bacterium. It could potentially multiply because it has no competition. In its decision to approve spinach and lettuce irradiation, the FDA even raised this issue. I went to the sources that they cited [in their approval] and they were just not convincing; there were not good studies to rule this hazard out. I think that's still a real issue."

Whom Is the Government Protecting?

In reading from the Centers for Disease Control website, one gets the impression that food irradiation is not only unharmful but beneficial. This is despite studies and other data that suggest otherwise.

"The government, as in many regulatory areas, has bought into industry arguments," Freese said. "I think they're favorable to irradiation when, in fact, they should be a lot more skeptical and be much more objective and scientific about it.

Two bunches of strawberries are shown here, several days after being picked. Irradiation has killed dangerous microorganisms in the berries on the left, increasing the fruit's shelf life, but critics say that irradiation also destroys important nutrients. (Cordelia Molloy/Photo Researchers, Inc.)

FDA Approval for Use of Food Irradiation

Product	Purpose	Date of Rule
Wheat and wheat powder	Disinfest insects	1963
White potatoes	Preservation	1965
Dry spices and seasonings	Decontamination/disinfest	1983
Pork and fresh non-cut processed cuts	Eliminate *Trichinella spiralis*	1985
Fresh fruits	Delay ripening	1986
Dry enzyme preparations	Decontamination	1986
Poultry	Pathogen reduction	1990
Red meat	Pathogen reduction	1997
Fresh shell eggs	*Salmonella* reduction	2000
Fresh lettuce and spinach	Pathogen reduction	2008

Taken from: *Environmental Public Health Today,* http://environmentalhealthtoday.wordpress.com/2009/05/08/food-irradiation-an-underutilized-food-safety-process.

"There are a lot of studies out there, and some of them do seem to suggest that irradiation is not a problem. But it's a case of the science not having captured all that's going on when you irradiate something. Sometimes the government will refer to studies from the 1990s that seem to show that irradiation is safe; yet in just this past decade new studies have come along that show previously undetected compounds appearing in irradiated foods, which have negative effects. There certainly needs to be more study done because there are troubling signs of toxicity. And there's no argument with the nutritional depletion—everybody knows that."

Deceiving Shoppers

Interestingly, while the government is insisting that irradiation is safe, the FDA recently proposed that labeling of irradiated foods—which currently must be done—be changed to make it less obvious. One has to wonder why, if irradiation is so safe, labeling needs to be restricted.

Currently, irradiated food must be labeled "Treated with irradiation" or "Treated by radiation" and must display the irradiated "radura" symbol. The new rule proposed by the FDA would allow irradiated food to be marketed in some cases without any labeling at all. In other cases, the rule would allow the terms *electronically pasteurized* or *cold pasteurized* to replace the use of *irradiated* on labels.

"This is totally unacceptable," Freese stated about the proposed change. "Irradiation has no scientific resemblance to pasteurization, which is a very well defined process used with milk. So it's clearly deception."

True Cause of Problems

Freese points out that irradiating foods is really an attempt to excuse food companies from having to clean up their manufacturing practices.

"Actually dealing with the true cause of these problems is really important," he said. "It's a shame. They've really fallen down on the job of policing these few huge slaughterhouses that process the majority of our meat. If you have any episode of contamination, even if it's pretty rare, it's going to affect a whole lot of people. And the standards at these plants are not what they should be. Basically we need to get away from this industrial agriculture and attack the problem at its source. At the least, higher standards would make these companies clean up their acts."

Fortunately, organizations such as CFS are in there fighting for both the "symptomatic cure" (food irradiation) and the actual cause itself.

Food Terrorism Is
a Serious Threat

Bill Marler

Bill Marler, a personal injury and products liability attorney who has been involved in many high-profile cases involving food-borne diseases, is a well-known advocate for food safety. In the following viewpoint Marler argues that America is ill-equipped to deal with a major food terrorism incident. He describes several successful food terrorism attacks that have already occurred and cites a Food and Drug Administration (FDA) report from 2003 that lists a number of food terrorism scenarios and indicates that there is a "high likelihood" of such an attack occurring. Marler claims that the Centers for Disease Control and Prevention and the FDA describe themselves as poorly prepared to deal with regular outbreaks of food-borne diseases, and thus he suggests they would be just as poorly equipped to deal with an intentional attack on the food supply.

SOURCE: Bill Marler, "Who Poisoned the Cookie Dough?" www.marler blog.com, June 27, 2009. Reproduced by permission of the author.

W hat if the cookie dough *E. coli* outbreak [in June 2009] actually happened this way?

At 10:00 PM last night between yet another story about Michael Jackson's death, a foreign Network begin airing a video taken inside a manufacturing facility showing someone treating a batch of cookie dough with an unknown liquid. There is a claim that this is a terrorist act.

In the next 15 minutes, every network news operation is playing the video. The broadcast networks break into regular programming to air it, and the cable news stations go nonstop with the video while talking heads dissect it. Michael Jackson fades into the distance.

Coming on a Friday evening on the East Coast, the food terrorism story catches the mainstream media completely off guard. Other than to say the video is being analyzed by CIA [Central Intelligence Agency] experts, and is presumed to be authentic, there isn't much coming out of the government.

Far-fetched? Don't count on it. I have been saying for years that a foodborne illness outbreak will look just like the terrorist act described above, but without the video on FOX News. Far-fetched?

Notable Food Terrorist Attacks

Tell that to the 751 people in Wasco County, Oregon— including 45 who required hospital stays—who in 1984 ate at any one of ten salad bars in town and were poisoned with *Salmonella* by followers of Bhagwan Shree Rajneesh. The goal was to make people who were not followers of the cult too sick to vote in county elections.

Tell that to Chile, where in 1989, a shipment of grapes bound for the United States was found laced with cyanide, bringing trade suspension that cost the South American country $200 million. It was very much like a 1970s plot by Palestinian terrorists to inject Israel's Jaffa oranges with mercury.

A grocery worker holds a box of Chilean fruit, which was banned in 1989 after the discovery in the United States of some cyanide-laced grapes from the South American country. The ensuing panic cost Chile about $200 million in lost trade. (Chuck Nacke/Time & Life Pictures/Getty Images)

Tell that to the 111 people, including 40 children, sickened in May 2003 when a Michigan supermarket employee intentionally tainted 200 pounds of ground beef with an insecticide containing nicotine. Tell that to Mr. Litvenenko, the Russian spy poisoned in the UK [United Kingdom] with polonium-laced food.

Tell that to Stanford University researchers who modeled a nightmare scenario where a mere 4 grams of botulinum toxin dropped into a milk production facility could cause serious illness and even death to 400,000 people in the United States.

Food Terrorism Is Very Likely

The reason I bring this up is not to mark another anniversary of 9/11, not because I actually think that food terrorism really is the cause of this week's *E. coli* cookie dough outbreak, but I wonder if it would have made any difference in our government's ability to figure out there was an outbreak, to figure out the cause, and to stop it before it sickened so many.

After 9/11, Health & Human Services Secretary Tommy G. Thompson said: "Public health is a national security issue. It must be treated as such. Therefore, we must not only make sure we can respond to a crisis, but we must make sure that we are secure in defending our stockpiles, our institutions and our products."

Before Thompson's early exit from the [George W.] Bush Administration, he did get published the "Risk Assessment for Food Terrorism and Other Food Safety Concerns." That document, now 5 years old, let the American public know that there is a "high likelihood" of food terrorism. It said the "possible agents for food terrorism" are:

> **FAST FACT**
>
> MSNBC reported in 2009 that the Food and Drug Administration currently inspects less than 1 percent of the food imported to the United States each year.

- Biological and chemical agents
- Naturally occurring, antibiotic-resistant, and genetically engineered substances
- Deadly agents and those tending to cause gastrointestinal discomfort
- Highly infectious agents and those that are not communicable
- Substances readily available to any individual and those more difficult to acquire, and
- Agents that must be weaponized and those accessible in a useable form.

After 9/11, Secretary Thompson said more inspectors and more traceability are keys to our food defense and safety. To date, we've made little movement to ensure this.

America Poorly Equipped to Deal with Food Terrorism

Would the fact of terrorists operating from inside a manufacturing facility somewhere inside the United States

Fear of Food Terrorism Is High

A large majority of Americans expect "deliberate chemical or biological contamination of a common food product" to occur during their lifetimes.

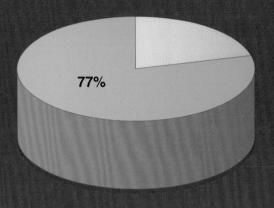

77%

Taken from: *Homeland Security Affairs*, Thomas F. Stinson et al. "How Would Americans Allocate Anti-terrorism Spending? Findings from a National Survey of Attitudes About Terrorism," June 2007.

bring more or effective resources to the search for the source of the *E. coli*? If credit-taking terrorists were putting poison on our cookies, could we be certain Uncle Sam's response would have been more robust or effective then if it was just a "regular" food illness outbreak?

Absolutely not! The CDC [Centers for Disease Control and Prevention] publicly admits that it manages to count and track only one of every forty foodborne illness victims, and that its inspectors miss key evidence as outbreaks begin. The FDA [Food and Drug Administration] is on record as referring to themselves as overburdened, underfunded, understaffed, and in possession of no real power to make a difference during recalls, because even Class 1 recalls are "voluntary." If you are a food manufacturer, packer, or distributor, you are more likely to be hit by lightning than be inspected by the FDA. You are perfectly free to continue to sell and distribute your poisoned product, whether it has been poisoned accidentally or intentionally.

The reality is that the cookie dough *E. coli* outbreak is a brutal object lesson in the significant gaps in our ability to track and protect our food supply. We are ill prepared for a crisis, regardless of who poisons us.

Somewhere between the farm and your table, our Uncle Sam got lost.

Food Terrorism Is Not a Serious Threat

Fred Burton and Scott Stewart

Fred Burton and Scott Stewart are counterterrorism experts with Stratfor, an intelligence agency that produces comprehensive reports on various terrorism and security-related threats. In the following viewpoint Burton and Stewart argue that the risk of a successful terrorist attack targeting the food supply is quite low. The authors discuss a number of food terrorist attacks that have occurred, noting that they did not succeed in killing or injuring very many people. They also claim that the agricultural system deals effectively with the types of pathogens that are likely to be used in such an attack, and that other features of the farming system would make a highly successful attack very unlikely. According to the authors, the fear response on the part of the public, in the unlikely event of a food terrorist incident, would probably vastly exceed actual deaths or injuries from the attack itself.

SOURCE: Fred Burton and Scott Stewart, "Placing the Terrorist Threat to the Food Supply in Perspective," www.stratfor.com, April 22, 2008. Reproduced by permission.

S ince the Sept. 11, 2001, attacks, there have been many reports issued by various government and civilian sources warning of the possibility that terrorists could target the U.S. food supply. At the most basic level, threats to a country's food supply can come in two general forms: attacks designed to create famine and attacks designed to directly poison people.

Attacks designed to create famine would entail the use of some agent intended to kill crops or livestock. Such agents could include pathogens, insects or chemicals. The pathogens might include such livestock diseases as *bovine* spongiform encephalopathy (BSE), commonly called mad cow disease, or hoof-and-mouth disease. Crop diseases such as Ug99 fungus or molds also pose a threat to supplies.

Attacks designed to poison people could also be further divided into two general forms: those intended to introduce toxins or pathogens prior to processing and those intended to attack finished food products. Attacks against foodstuffs during agricultural production could include placing an agent on crops in the field or while in transit to a mill or processing center. Attacks against finished foodstuffs would entail covertly placing the toxin or pathogen into the finished food product after processing.

It must be noted that an attack against people could also be conducted for the purposes of creating a mass disruption—such action would not be designed to cause mass casualties, but rather to create fear, unrest and mistrust of the government and food supply, or to promote hoarding. In fact, based on historical examples of incidents involving the contamination of food products, such an attack is far more likely to occur than a serious systematic attack on the food supply.

A Productive Food Terrorism Attack Is Difficult

While attacks against the food supply may appear simple in theory, they have occurred infrequently and for good reason: When one considers the sheer size of the U.S. agricultural sector, conducting a productive assault proves difficult.

As seen by the coca and marijuana eradication efforts by the United States and its partners in Mexico, Central America and the Andes, the logistical effort needed to make any substantial dent in agricultural production is massive. Even the vast resources the United States has dedicated to drug eradication tasks in small countries—overt plane flights spraying untold thousands of gallons of herbicides for decades—have failed to create more than a limited effect on marijuana and coca crops. Obviously, any sort of meaningful chemical attack on U.S. agriculture would have to be so massive that it is simply not logistically feasible.

This is where pathogens—agents that can, at least in theory, be introduced in limited amounts, reproduce and then rapidly spread to infect a far larger area—enter the picture. In order to be effective, however, a pathogen must be one that is easily spread and very deadly and has a long incubation period (in order to ensure it is passed along before the host dies). It is also very helpful to the propagation of a disease if it is difficult to detect and/or difficult to treat. While a pathogen that possesses all of the aforementioned traits could be devastating, finding such an agent is difficult. Few diseases have all the requisite characteristics. Some are very deadly, but act too quickly to be passed, while others are more readily passed but do not have a long incubation period or are not as virulent. Other pathogens, such as the Ug99 wheat fungus, are easy to detect and kill. There is also the problem of mutation, meaning that many pathogens tend to mutate into less virulent actors. It is also important to note that genetically engineering a super bug—one that possesses

FAST FACT

The National Center for Food Protection and Defense reports that Americans want most antiterrorist spending to be on food-supply protection, despite considering other forms of terrorism more likely.

all the characteristics to make it highly effective—is still much harder in real life than it is on television.

Even if such an effective pathogen is found, someone intending to use it in an attack must isolate the virulent strain, manufacture it in sufficient quantities to be effective, ship it to the place of the planned attack and then distribute it in a manner whereby it is effectively dispersed. The infrastructure required to undertake such an endeavor is both large and expensive. Even in past cases where groups possessed the vast monetary resources to fund biological weapons efforts and amassed the scientific expertise to attempt such a program—Aum Shinrikyo [a Japanese cult responsible for a high-profile terrorist nerve gas attack in 1995] comes to mind—virulent pathogens have proven very difficult to produce and effectively disperse in large quantities.

The Agricultural System Deals Effectively with Pathogens

Another factor making these sorts of attacks difficult to orchestrate is the very nature of farming. For thousands of years, farmers have been battling plant and animal diseases. Most of the pathogens that are mentioned in connection with attacks against agriculture include elements already existing in nature, such as hoof-and-mouth disease, H5N1 bird flu or a fungus like Ug99. As a result, farmers and governmental organizations such as the Animal and Plant Health Inspection Service have systems in place to monitor crops and animals for signs of pathogens. When these pathogens appear, action is taken and diseased crops are treated or eradicated. Animals are treated or culled. Even in past cases where massive eradication and culling efforts occurred—BSE in the United Kingdom, citrus canker in Florida or the many bird flu outbreaks over the past few years—the measures have not crippled or affected the country's agricultural sector or the larger economy.

Creating famine and poisoning the food supply are also difficult, given the sheer quantity of agricultural products grown. Applying some sort of toxin before the raw food is processed is difficult, given the volume produced. In fact, much grain is diverted to uses other than human consumption, as when corn is used to produce ethanol or feed livestock. Therefore, if a truckload of corn is poisoned, it might never funnel into the human food chain. Furthermore, even if a truck of contaminated grain were destined for the food chain, by the time it made its way through the process it would likely be too diluted to have any effect. During the production process, contaminated corn would first have to combine with other grain, sit in a silo, be moved and stored again, ground and finally made into a finished food product such as a loaf of cornbread—an unlikely source of poisoning for the end user. Processing, washing, cooking, pasteurizing and refining may all also serve to further dilute, cleanse or damage the pathogen in the targeted product. At this point, food is also inspected for naturally occurring pathogens and toxins. Such inspections could help spot an intentional contamination.

Besides, even contaminating one truckload of grain would require a large amount of toxin. Producing that much toxin would require a substantial infrastructure—one that would require a great deal of time and money to build. Not to mention the difficulty inherent in transporting and delivering the toxin.

Past Attacks Prove Rare

Actual attacks against food are very rare. And due to the considerations enumerated above, nearly every food attack we are aware of was an attempt to directly poison people and not cause famine. Furthermore, almost all of these attacks involved processed foods or raw foods packaged for human consumption.

While people are frequently sickened by pathogens in food such as *E. coli* or *Salmonella* bacteria, most incidents

are not intentional. One of the few known successful attempts at using a biological agent to contaminate food in the United States occurred in 1984 in the small Oregon town of The Dalles. Followers of cult leader Bhagwan Shree Rajneesh, attempting to manipulate a local election, infected salad bars in 10 restaurants with *Salmonella typhimurium,* causing about 751 people to become ill.

A second contamination attempt occurred in October 1996, when 12 laboratory workers at a large medical center in Texas experienced severe gastrointestinal illness after eating muffins and doughnuts left in their break room. Laboratory tests revealed that the pastries had been intentionally infected with S. dysenteriae, a pathogen that rarely occurs in the United States. An investigation later determined that the pathogen came from a stock culture kept at the lab.

While many people recall the 1989 Chilean grape scare—when two grapes imported to the United States

One of the most successful food terrorism attacks in the United States occurred in Oregon in 1984, when followers of Bhagwan Shree Rajneesh (right) sprayed *Salmonella* bacteria on salad bars in ten restaurants, causing hundreds of people to fall ill. (Jack Smith/AP Images)

were injected with cyanide—few recall that the perpetrator in the case made several calls to the U.S. Embassy warning of the contamination and was therefore not seriously attempting to harm people, but rather attempting an action designed to draw attention to social injustice in Chile. The warning calls allowed agricultural inspectors to find the damaged and discolored grapes before they were eaten.

In a lesser-known case that took place in 1978, a dozen children in the Netherlands and West Germany were hospitalized after eating oranges imported from Israel. The Arab Revolutionary Council, a nom de guerre [pseudonym] used by the Abu Nidal Organization, deliberately contaminated the fruit with mercury in an attempt to damage the Israeli economy.

Potential Players and the Public Impact

Such attacks could potentially be conducted by a wide array of actors, ranging from a single mentally disturbed individual on one end of the spectrum to sovereign nations on the other end. Cults and domestic or transnational terrorist groups fall somewhere in the middle. The motivation behind these diverse actors could range from monetary extortion or attempts to commit mass murder to acts of war designed to cripple the U.S. economy or the nation's ability to project power.

Of these actors, however, there are very few who possess the ability to conduct attacks that could have a substantial impact on the U.S. food supply. In fact, most of the actors are only capable of contaminating finished food products. While they all have this rudimentary capability, there is also the question of intent.

Documents and manuals found in Afghanistan after the 2001 U.S.-led invasion revealed an al Qaeda interest in conducting chemical and biological attacks, although this interest was not a well-developed program. From a cost-benefit standpoint, it would be much cheaper and easier to use explosives to create disruption than it would be to execute a complicated plot against the food supply. Besides, such a target would not produce the type of spectacular imagery the group enjoys.

While we do not foresee any huge attempt by the Russians or Chinese, and food supply is not a part of al Qaeda's preferred target set, it is possible that a lone wolf or a smaller extremist organization could attempt to conduct such an attack. While any such offensive will likely have limited success, it could have far wider societal repercussions. At the present time, the public has become somewhat accustomed to food scares and recalls over things such as contaminated spinach, ground beef and green onions. Even warnings over lead and other harmful chemicals in food imported from China have caused concern. However, if even a relatively unsuccessful attack on the food supply were conducted by a terrorist group, it could create significant hysteria—especially if the media sensationalized the event. In such a case, even an ineffective terror plot could result in a tremendous amount of panic and economic loss.

The Fear Response Is Exaggerated

Perhaps the best recent example of this type of disruptive attack is the 2001 anthrax letter attacks. Although the attacks only claimed the lives of five victims, they caused a huge, disproportionate effect on the collective American and world psyche. The public fears that arose from the anthrax attacks were augmented by extensive media discussions about the use of the agent as a weapon. The public sense of unease was further heightened by the fact that the perpetrator was never identified or apprehended. As a result, countless instances surfaced in which irrational panic caused office buildings, apartment buildings, government offices and factories to be evacuated. Previously ignored piles of drywall dust and the powdered sugar residue left by someone who ate a donut at his desk led to suspicions about terrorists, who suddenly seemed to be lurking around every corner. It did not matter, in the midst of the fear, that the

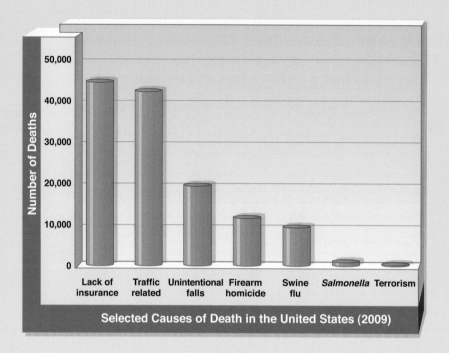

Number of Deaths

50,000
40,000
30,000
20,000
10,000
0

Lack of insurance | Traffic related | Unintentional falls | Firearm homicide | Swine flu | *Salmonella* | Terrorism

Selected Causes of Death in the United States (2009)

Taken from: http://firedoglake.com.

place where the "anthrax" was found could have absolutely no symbolic or strategic value to the Islamist militants that most Americans pictured in their minds. The sense of threat and personal vulnerability was pervasive.

In the years since 2001, thousands of hoax anthrax letters have been sent to companies, government offices, schools and politicians in the United States and abroad. Many of these hoaxes have caused psychosomatic responses, resulting in victims being hospitalized, and further economic losses in terms of lost production time, emergency hazmat response costs and laboratory tests.

In the end, the most probable attack against the food supply is unlikely to create a significant death toll, but the panic such an attack may evoke can cause repercussions that are far greater than the death toll itself.

CHAPTER 3

Personal Experiences with Food-Borne Diseases

A Female College Student Survives an *E. coli* Infection

Lauren

Lauren is a college student who wrote a report about her food-borne disease experience for S.T.O.P. (Safe Tables Our Priority), a national, nonprofit, public health organization dedicated to preventing illness and death from food-borne pathogens. In the following account Lauren says that a couple of days after eating a spinach salad she developed symptoms that at first seemed flulike, but became much worse over time. She reports that eventually she realized she had to go to the emergency room, where after many tests and misdiagnoses it was discovered that she had become infected with *E. coli* O157:H7, the deadliest strain of *E. coli*.

Loneliness, frustration, and fear were the last emotions I ever expected to feel as I began my junior year of college. Leaving school, living at home with my parents, and cloudy thoughts of dying were far beyond anything I could have ever imagined. I had never done drugs, drank in excess, or even missed a home-

Photo on previous page. Just about every food-borne disease has symptoms of abdominal cramps, diarrhea, and vomiting. (LADA/Photo Researchers, Inc.)

SOURCE: Lauren Bush, "*E coli* O157H7," www.safetables.org, 2009. Reproduced by permission.

work assignment; but within 48 hours of consuming a small spinach salad I found myself in this unfortunate position. . . .

The afternoon of my first day of classes on Wednesday August 23 I stood in our small kitchen eating a small spinach salad with tomatoes and poppy seed dressing chatting with my new roommates. The next two days of classes continued normally, but that Saturday morning when I awoke I felt strange. The closest illness I knew to identify with my symptoms was the flu because I felt nauseous, with body aches and chills. My first instinct was to call my mother and tell her that I didn't feel well and ask what she thought about my symptoms. She told me to rest, do the usual sick regimen like drinking plenty of fluids and see how I felt the next morning. Even though it was the middle of the day, I felt so weak I couldn't do anything but sleep. That night I went to bed hoping that

The author's *E. coli* infection resulted from her eating spinach from California that was contaminated with the bacteria. (Eric Albrecht/AP Images)

the next morning I would feel better, only to begin the first night of many terrible nights to come.

Intense Pain and Diarrhea

The pain in my stomach grew and seemed to settle into one burning spot that I couldn't escape from, no matter which way I twisted or turned throughout the night. Then, the diarrhea began. During that one endless night I was forced to jump from bed and run into the bathroom 11 or 12 times. It may have gone on longer, but I lost count after that point. At age 20 I was so unable to hold it that a few times I didn't make it to the bathroom before I lost control of my faculties. The next morning, I got up very early and forced myself to dress so that I could drive to the urgent treatment center where I had been in the past. No one I knew was around to take me and I was so blinded by the pain that I just left without remembering my cell phone.

Squirming on the hard plastic chair, counting the seconds until I was called back to the examining room, I had to keep running to the bathroom in the waiting room. When I was finally called back, I was forced to wait again. Unable to sit up, I lay back on the table and fell asleep. I have no idea how long I laid there before the doctor arrived. After a few questions she began pushing on my abdomen and when I cried out in pain, she told me she was almost positive that I had appendicitis and needed to go immediately to the emergency room [ER]. I felt like I was dreaming, but I slid off of the table and made my way back to the waiting room. As I stood there paying, I realized with dread that I didn't have my cell phone and the treatment center didn't have long distance service, so I wasn't able to call any of my friends to come get me. So I made my way, slowly and painfully, to my car and drove back to my house where I ran into one of my roommates. When I asked if she could take me to the ER she said that she had to go to work, so I found my cell phone and left, alone. Driving to the ER I called my family and then my boyfriend who happened to be out of town that day. Sobbing and in tremendous pain I parked and made my way into my second waiting room that day. I waited for over an hour on another hard plastic chair, with my eyes closed, trying not to breathe because of the pain. After what seemed like a lifetime I was finally called to be examined.

The nurse determined that I had a fever and put me in a second waiting room for the doctor. A young, attractive man entered and I had to describe, completely embarrassed, everything that had happened thus far. After 6 hours of laying on a small bed behind a curtain the staff had drawn blood, taken a urine sample, done an MRI [magnetic resonance imaging] and tried to take a stool sample. . . .

The ER doctor had given me dicyclomine to slow my stomach cramps, which gave me the first relief I had in 2 days. By this time my parents were driving to be with me, but they lived over 3 hours away, so about the time I was ready to be discharged, they arrived. It was determined at this point that I didn't have appendicitis and simply a bad stomach virus. Driving me back to my house, my parents slept with me in my room that night, watching over me carefully. . . .

The Worst Seemed to Be Over

During the time that I felt better, I convinced my parents to return home. I was feeling much better and it seemed like the worst was over. After I called my mother to tell her that something was very, very wrong my father returned to find me in too much pain to walk, so he carried me out to his truck. After a long, miserable ride home we met my mother at an urgent treatment clinic. I had never been in a hospital, broken a bone or even had an I.V. started up until this point in my life. I remember being terrified of having an I.V. in my arm, but I needed fluids because I was so dehydrated from all of the diarrhea. Since it was so late, and many of the departments were closed, they administered Demerol [a painkiller] and sent me home to return in the morning. The next morning, still hemorrhaging, we returned to the clinic for more tests. I was put in a wheelchair because it hurt so much to walk. I had another MRI, X-rays, blood work, the list goes on. When nothing could be determined, the clinic admitted me to the hospital. I sobbed through the whole conversation with the doctor and through the ride to the hospital, what was wrong with me!?! Was I dying?

FAST FACT

According to the Centers for Disease Control and Prevention, up to 16 percent of victims in some *E. coli* 0157:H7 outbreaks have developed hemolytic uremic syndrome, which can cause kidney failure and death.

After being admitted the staff administered more pain medication and started the real battery of tests: stool samples, many more MRIs, more blood work, enemas, nuclear testing, ultrasounds, pushing and prodding. All food was stopped in an effort to find the real source of the trauma and pain. I am a small person and my veins were unable to withstand so much of so many different drugs. One long, miserable night my I.V. had begun to back up and my vein collapsed, so the nurses began hunting for a new vein. My mother finally made them stop after 13 sticks and the next morning I was wheeled, terrified, to an operating room where a team made an incision in my right arm and inserted a PICC (peripherally inserted central [catheter]) line, where a catheter is inserted in a vein close to one's heart so that my veins could rest and the same medicine could be administered.

After 2 days of no developments and a team of doctors and specialists working on my case, a surgeon entered my room in the evening. In my hazy, drug induced state I remember him telling my family and me that he would have to remove my colon in order to stop the hemorrhaging and any further problems if I didn't improve. I remember being so devastated that I let the drugs push me into a deep sleep, while my, parents leaned over me crying. It was by far the scariest moment in my entire young life.

Shocking Lab Results

However, through an IV barrage of the most powerful drugs available over the next 3 days, I did improve greatly. Then, to our shock and surprise, the news returned to us from the [lab]—the culture revealed that I had ingested H157, the worst [strain] of *E coli*. After a total of 6 days in the hospital, I was released to go home with instructions to continue taking potassium and eat a gentle diet. My family and I hoped that this was the end, but unfortunately it wasn't. Less than one week later, similar symptoms began occurring and I was again admitted to the hospital. After another week in the hospital, several more tests and another PICC line, it was determined that I had *Clostridium difficile* from the plethora of antibiotic drugs launched on my system because all of the bacteria, both good and bad, had been expelled from my system. With more medicine and a daily schedule of yogurt to provide good bacteria, I was able to go home and continue recovering.

During my recovery at home none of my sorority sisters and neither of my roommates called to ask how I was doing or the details of what had happened. It felt as though I had vanished from my own life, like I had died, but was granted the ability to watch my funeral and discover that no one came. Many people in my community where I grew up sent flowers or stopped by to say hello, but I was stricken by this feeling of abandonment and while I was still at home I wrote a letter explaining my choice to permanently leave the organization. To make matters worse, even though I still paid the rent, I refused to pay the utilities for a space I was not using, so my roommates and I shared a frosty existence over the next several months after my return until I was able to move out into an apartment of my own.

I ate spinach on August 23rd, 2006. I became violently sick on August 26th. I was in recovery until January, 2007. In many ways, I am still recovering and my life was altered in more ways than anyone could ever understand and this was a small part of my story.

A Mother Loses Her Son to Variant Creutzfeldt-Jakob Disease

Sandra Dick

Sandra Dick is the chief writer at the *Edinburgh Evening News* in Scotland. She graduated from Napier University with a degree in journalism. In the following viewpoint Dick interviews a mother who lost her son to a rare food-borne disease called variant Creutzfeldt-Jakob disease (vCJD), which is sometimes incorrectly referred to as mad cow disease. Mad cow disease affects cattle (its official name is bovine spongiform encephalopathy, or BSE); people get variant CJD by eating beef from cows infected with BSE. The boy's mother helplessly watched her twenty-year-old son, a strong, healthy young man, suffer and die from this degenerative brain disease. The disease had been incubating in his system for about ten years, she tells us, but it is so rare that at first health-care providers did not know what was wrong with him or how to help him.

SOURCE: Sandra Dick, "CJD RIPS You to Bits . . . It Is Unstoppable," *Edinburgh Evening News,* Oct. 30, 2009, p. 20. Copyright © 2009 Johnston Publishing Ltd. Reproduced by permission.

It was the food crisis of the nineties and, like every other mum, Kate Madden had watched the BSE [bovine spongiform encephalopathy] crisis unfold with horror.

Images of cows staggering from pen to pen, government ministers feeding burgers to their children while insisting all was fine and scientists predicting a nightmare faced by patients and families affected by its human form.

Variant CJD [Creutzfeldt-Jakob disease]—a brain condition linked to eating infected meat—was the biggest health scare in a decade.

Mums like Kate, with two hungry boys to feed, couldn't help but wonder what exactly was going into their favourite foods.

A False Sense of Security

A decade on and BSE was supposed to have been dealt with, as nightmare scenarios of hundreds falling victim to 'human form' vCJD didn't appear to have come true. Burgers, sausages and meat pies were back on the menu.

So how then—and why—was Kate's strapping son now dying from it?

"He was 6 ft 1 in tall, he weighed 15 stone [210 pounds], he was going into the Army," says Kate, eyes flashing with hurt, anger and bitterness from behind her auburn fringe as she tells how she watched her son's horrific death.

"He'd been accepted to do his basic training," she proudly adds. "He was fit, healthy. He didn't smoke, he hardly drank.

"Why was this happening to him?"

Kate clutches a handful of photographs of Alan which reveal a strong young man with an open smile. Some show him in playful mood, arms wrapped round relatives and friends, one has him posing proudly in his blue

> **FAST FACT**
>
> Whereas Creutzfeldt-Jakob disease typically affects people over sixty, the Washington State Department of Health reported in 2010 that variant Creutzfeldt-Jakob disease affects people at a much younger age—victims of this rare disease are often in their twenties or, in some cases, even teenagers.

Air Cadet uniform, a snapshot of the military man he wanted to be and which, tragically, would eventually appear on the front of his funeral order of service.

Then come the snaps [photos] of 20-year-old Alan taken just a few weeks after he was finally diagnosed as a one-in-a-million bad luck case, one of Britain's small but disturbing number of vCJD victims.

They show his muscular body already wasting away—he'd eventually weigh less than eight stone [136 pounds]—the wide grin replaced by a blank expression.

Later he's pictured in a wheelchair and lying in a hospital bed with padded sides to stop him smacking his face against the metal frame as his body was wracked by uncontrollable jerks. He's blind and he's mute, he's lost control of his bodily functions and he's dying.

Kate is pictured with him, face ghostly white and her sunken eyes pleading, arms wrapped around her son who, in just four hellish months, had deteriorated in front of her and who would soon die in her arms.

A Horrific Death

"He died in a truly horrific way," she says in a whisper. "I work in healthcare, I've seen people die and some go peacefully and quietly.

"Alan didn't. When he died his face was pinched into this horrific expression. He was yellow—his liver and kidneys had stopped working.

"He didn't look to me like he was at peace."

She's speaking out about her son's death last June [2008] in the run-up to National CJD Day on 12 November, an event aimed at reminding healthcare professionals and the public that the legacy of the nineties' BSE crisis is with us today, as well as highlighting the plight of families affected by various forms of Creutzfeldt-Jakob disease (CJD).

For like most of us she thought the nightmare headlines of hundreds of people dying as the result of eating infected meat would never affect her family and that vCJD was last decade's problem.

A cow infected with bovine spongiform encephalopathy (BCE) is shown here. Variant Creutzfeldt-Jakob disease, a serious and usually fatal brain disorder, is caused by eating beef cattle with BSE. (C.E.V./Photo Researchers, Inc.)

"It's not something you ever think is going to happen," says Kate, 47, originally from Wales but who has lived with partner Jim Watson, 45, in Loanhead [Scotland] for two years. "You end up with so many questions. I couldn't understand why one of my sons had it but the other didn't. What was it that meant Alan had this?"

His brother, Richard, 28, raised the alarm after collecting Alan for a family funeral. "He looked like a tramp," explains Kate. "Richard thought he was having a breakdown.

"On the way home Alan was holding his hand over his eye the whole time. Richard phoned me and I wondered if he might have had a stroke."

In fact, her son's condition was linked to the horrors of the BSE "mad cow" crisis and he'd been incubating his illness for around ten years.

But so unusual is the condition—in the 13 years since the first vCJD cases there have been 165 deaths—that medical staff were also caught out. It took two painful weeks to diagnose what was happening and even then, Kate says that it seemed as if no-one really knew how to care for Alan.

She was told his condition would take around a year to progress. In fact he deteriorated at a rapid pace as his brain turned sponge-like and he was robbed of the ability to carry out the most basic functions.

An Incredible Guilt

To add to her distress, Kate was quizzed by a researcher from [the United Kingdom] Creutzfeldt-Jakob Disease Surveillance Unit based in Edinburgh, who wanted to know what kind of food her son had eaten as a child, raising dreadful feelings of guilt and fear.

"Families affected by vCJD feel incredible guilt, they feel they have failed their youngsters and they can't understand why it has happened to them," explains Gill Turner of the CJD Support Network.

"They are tormented. They remember how they all shared the same food. When you think you are giving someone a good meal and then this happens . . . it's tragic."

Kate was with Alan in Wales when he died last June—the sole victim of vCJD in 2008.

"There had been talk for weeks about getting him out of hospital and into a flat. He was in it for just eight days when he died," she remembers.

"He was in a terrible state. I crawled into bed beside him and cuddled him. There was nothing anyone could do—this disease rips people to bits, you can't stop it, you can't make them better and you can't take it away."

Today her most precious reminder of her son is a poignant text message he sent her—one of the last he ever sent—during an amazingly lucid moment just after Mother's Day in March last year.

"Could you come and see me please?" it reads. "I want to see my cats, I want to go and live and to do stuff.

"I love you."

A Family Is Poisoned by a Common Bean Toxin

Vicky Jones

Vicky Jones is a food writer and author of *The House and Garden Cookbook*. In the following account she reports that she likes to experiment in the kitchen, and one night she was modifying a recipe by substituting different beans and using a different cooking method. Within a few hours of consuming the meal, first her brother, then her husband, then she herself became very ill. She explains that she eventually realized that she had accidentally poisoned her family and herself with a toxin commonly found in raw beans. Jones relates their ordeal and the important lessons she learned from it.

I t was only when my husband started vomiting too that the horrible truth dawned on me—both he and my brother, who had dropped by for dinner, must have food poisoning. And another horrible thought rapidly followed, namely that I must be responsible. Moi? Impossible.

SOURCE: Vicky Jones, "Beware of the Beans: How Beans Can Be a Surprising Source of Food Poisoning," www.independent.co.uk, Sept. 16, 2008. Reproduced by permission.

All of the likely suspects ran through my mind: eggs, chicken, fish, rice, or could it be lettuce? Highly unlikely, but dim memories of a food hygiene course I'd once attended produced the thought that salad leaves could be the culprit. The meal had been vegan, so no animal products could be to blame, and we hadn't eaten rice.

By now, things were moving fast, literally, and both our loos [bathrooms] were permanently occupied. Feeling relieved that at least I was OK, I rushed from one to the other, offering feeble consolation and wondering what to do, as both men seemed to be getting rapidly worse, their faces changing from virulent red to ash grey and then to white in quick succession. Whatever the offending substance, their bodies just wanted to get rid of it by whatever means possible. Clearly, they were both very ill.

Undercooked Beans Were the Culprit

While I found bowls and towels and coaxed my husband and brother up to bed, I continued to rack my brains. Then it dawned on me—it must have been the beans. I admit to having a weakness for experimenting in the kitchen, and that evening had made *ta'amia,* or falafel, from a recipe in Claudia Roden's erudite and revered *Middle Eastern Food,* except that I didn't have the dried white broad beans found in Greek shops that she recommends. But I did have some dried and soaked Greek butter beans, the ones known as gigantes (because they're so huge), so I thought I'd use those instead as they looked very similar. Instead of boiling the beans first, then making patties and frying them, this Egyptian recipe uses ground raw beans, which are then deep fried. I made two fatal flaws: I used different beans from those specified in the recipe and I shallow fried, instead of deep frying.

In Israel, the rissoles are known as falafel, and are made with dried chickpeas instead of broad beans, again by soaking the pulse [beans], then grinding it into a paste, then deep-frying the rissoles in hot oil. Sometimes a mixture of dried broad beans and chickpeas are used, both of which have been grown, like lentils, in the Middle East since time immemorial—unlike the kidney beans, butter beans and cannellini beans we know today, which arrived in Europe only with the conquistadores. So the large butter beans I used came from a different family from the ones specified in the recipe, and turned out to have very different properties, too.

The *ta'amia* tasted delicious, crisply fried and aromatic with cumin and coriander, and flecked with bright

The food-poisoning ordeal of the author and her family began when she undercooked butter beans, which contain a virulent toxin. (Monkey Business Images/www.Shutter stock.com)

green parsley. Everybody enjoyed them, asking for second helpings, even. Within two hours of eating this fateful meal, I was also retching and vomiting, accompanied by the runs, and feeling like death.

From my bed I managed to phone NHS [National Health Service] Direct, in the hope of getting reassurance that although severely ill, we would recover quickly and that no treatment was necessary. No such reassurance was forthcoming, and another hour elapsed before I had another go at contacting the outside world, this time phoning our GP's [general practitioner's] emergency number. Eventually I spoke to a doctor, who was on the phone when my husband moaned that he was vomiting blood. On hearing this, the doctor told me to call an ambulance.

Many Raw Beans Are Toxic

The ambulance arrived an hour later. We live in a remote farmhouse which is hard to find at the best of times, and nearly impossible for ambulance drivers unfamiliar with dark lanes and equipped only with third-hand directions. Although very, very kind and helpful, the ambulance drivers were not paramedics and had no drugs on board. All they could do was to take us to hospital. When we explained the problem, they contacted a poisons unit in the hope of getting some information about the toxic properties of beans, but this was to no avail. After 20 minutes, the poisons unit phoned back to say they could shed no further light on the condition.

When forced to decide whether to be taken in to A&E [Accident & Emergency], where no doubt we'd spend all night waiting, we separately and collectively chose to remain at home. By now, death seemed preferable to hospital. And anyway, who'd look after the dog?

By the morning we'd all recovered enough to hold down water, and though unable to wake up properly, we knew we were on the mend. Later, research by a doctor-friend unearthed information from the US Food and Drug Administration website, which identifies the toxin as a lectin or phytohemagglutinin, found in many species of bean but in its highest concentration in the red kidney bean.

It's widely known that these beans should be boiled vigorously for 15 minutes to destroy the toxin before simmering, but I didn't know that cannellini or white kidney beans also contain this toxin—about one-third of the amount of the red ones. The butter beans I used contain it, too, as, indeed, do broad beans, though the latter only in quantities of between 5 per cent and 10 per cent of those found in red kidney beans. And cooking beans constantly at low temperature, as in a slow cooker, can increase their toxicity five-fold. So by shallow frying my rissoles, rather than deep frying them, as specified in the recipe, I probably made them even more poisonous than if they were eaten raw.

This syndrome is not well known in the medical community, and many cases must be misdiagnosed or never reported, as no figures of reported cases seem to be available. The National Poisons Information Service is available only to health professionals, and members of the public must rely on NHS Direct or their GP. But the database they use doesn't flag up the dangers of white beans as well as red, and what about pink, brown, green or mottled ones?

The message is this: soak any beans, whatever colour, in water for 12 hours, pour away the water, then boil briskly in fresh water for at least 15 minutes before cooking further. And if you do repeat my mistake, and make yourself ill, recovery is usually rapid—three to four hours after the onset of symptoms—and spontaneous.

FAST FACT

The Food and Drug Administration reports that levels of the toxin phytohemagglutinin in red kidney beans are so high that as few as four raw beans can trigger poisoning symptoms.

A Man Suffers a Case of *Salmonella* Food Poisoning

Anonymous

The author of this account is an anonymous contributor to www.foodpoisoningprevention.com, a website created by Michael Doom to disseminate information on food-borne diseases. In the following viewpoint the author describes an experience with *Salmonella* food poisoning. According to Doom, the symptoms appeared when he was driving home and quickly became so severe that he required medical attention. The author discusses how his doctor and other health-care workers were able to track down the cause of the illness and describes his gradual recovery over a period of a few days. Doom worked as a Registered Environmental Health Specialist for Los Angeles County for over twenty-one years and is an expert on food safety, sanitation, and food poisoning prevention.

It began with a small stomach cramp. Then after just what seemed like a few minutes, the cramps became much more severe, almost like a grumbling, and I felt the beginning of a nauseating feeling, which I knew was telling me I might have to throw up soon.

SOURCE: "A Common Food Poisoning Story," www.foodpoisoningprevention.com. Reproduced by permission.

Fortunately, I was close to home when the severe cramps and nausea started. I pulled into my driveway. Quickly got out, which was not a good idea since as soon as I stood up, the "might have to throw up" turned to "have to throw up" within the next minute or less.

I quickly made it to the door, unlocked it and just made it to the toilet to release whatever was in my system, at least the top part.

After a few minutes of vomiting my lunch (it was about 7 PM and I hadn't eaten anything since lunch), my body didn't believe my stomach when it kept saying there is nothing left. I almost missed the other symptom.

Severe cramps are to diarrhea what nausea is to vomiting—a warning that something wants to get out!

I wasn't quite finished throwing up so I grabbed the trash can near by, pulled down my pants and quickly turned around to sit on the toilet, almost all in one very quick motion (sorry if you can you picture this).

This is where I remained, even though my stomach and intestines kept expressly saying that there was not one molecule of organic or inorganic matter left.

I remember only praying in between the small breaks in pain. Nothing else occupied my mind until I heard someone come in. All I could say in between moans was "HELP"!!

The Symptoms Came On Quickly

I was told that I was there for probably an hour. My wife finally came home and found me moaning on the toilet. She helped clean me up and move to the bed. When I tried to stand up, I felt the other symptoms, which surprised me because my brain was still occupied on the first ones. Chills and a definite fever.

How could this be happening so quickly, I remember thinking. I felt perfectly fine just a short time ago.

I slowly crawled into bed and attempted to take off my clothes and put on some PJs. I knew as soon as I [lay] down that this was going to be temporary. The short break was over and I needed to get back to my "throne". My wife helped me up and back to the bathroom again just in time.

This became the routine for the next 24 hours, with the wife attempting to give me small sips of tea and water, none of which stayed down for very long.

My wife called the doctor who basically told her to continue giving small amounts of liquids and try to rest. "Bring him into the office in the morning if nothing changed."

Great I thought . . . no drug, no cure, just wallow in your pain all night.

You never realize how long nights can be until you experience a painful illness that will not allow you to sleep. None of the normal time killing distractions work very well when you're in that much pain.

In the morning the wife packed what little was left of me into the car with the gear needed to catch anything I might dispel, and off to the doctor's office we went. I didn't realize how bumpy our streets are (actually they are quite smooth). When you're weak, the muscles you normally depend on are just absent.

Looking for the Cause

After literally dragging myself into the doctor's office and trying to get comfortable (impossible at this point), the nursing assistant finally came in and asked me a lot of questions; symptoms, when they first appeared, types of pains, any blood in the stool (not that I saw) and more, and what I had eaten the past few meals. That's easy . . . nothing! Actually she said before the symptoms started.

Normally, when I'm healthy I can't remember what I had eaten during the day. How can I remember now when pain is clouding everything? I gave her as much as I could going back to breakfast and dinner the day before. After documenting all this, taking my temperature, blood pressure etc. she left and a few minutes later the doctor came in. After reading my responses he asked a few more questions and then proceeded to poke me in a few areas and take a stool and blood sample. I had been so cleansed, I don't know how he could even find anything to examine.

He said it was most likely something I had eaten and the symptoms will probably go away on their own by later today or tonight. He didn't want to prescribe any antibiotics, at least not right now, until the tests come back. He can prescribe an anti-vomiting and diarrhea medication or recommend one off the shelf at the pharmacy. But I may not keep it down long enough to make a difference.

If the symptoms continue and I'm not able to keep any liquids down, the next step would be to be admitted to the hospital to start an intravenous line to help re-hydrate me.

I passed on all this and said I might try something off the shelf at the drug store.

After what appeared to be a worthless trip to the doctor, I struggled back home and climbed back into bed. First though, one more visit to the toilet. I decided not to take any drugs and to keep drinking or sipping fluids.

> ## FAST FACT
>
> Each year *Salmonella* bacteria cause an estimated 1.4 million cases of food-borne disease and five hundred deaths in the United States, according to the Centers for Disease Control and Prevention.

The Symptoms Start to Improve

To my surprise, the doctor was right, I did start to feel almost human by the evening and was able to actually eat some soup and drink some water. The symptoms had begun to disappear almost as quickly as they had begun. I have experienced similar symptoms before with the flu, but never with such speed of onset, continuous pain and then quick conclusion. . . .

The doctor called the next day to let me know that the lab came back with a positive for *Salmonella* in my stool. I had contracted the *Salmonella* bacteria probably from

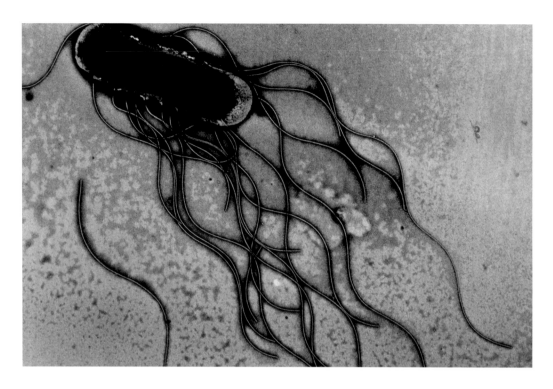

Salmonella, a rod-shaped bacterium, caused the author's illness. Such infections can be fatal. (Science Source/Photo Researchers, Inc.)

the breakfast on the day I experienced the symptoms, or from the dinner the night before. In any case he said that since I was feeling much better, he wasn't going to prescribe anything but he would like to get another stool sample in a week or so to see if the *Salmonella* bacteria is still hanging around. (Normal healthy people can become carriers for *Salmonella,* as well as many other nasty organisms.)

He also mentioned that someone from the county public health department would be contacting me to ask a lot of questions to try to locate the source.

I had forgotten that the nursing assistant had asked about my last few meals and so I started thinking back again and remembered something that escaped me during my incapacitation.

I had gone out to breakfast that morning to a local restaurant I had eaten at countless times before, and had ordered scrambled eggs. Again, something I had done countless times before without any problems. This time though the eggs seemed runny or undercooked, and only warm. I didn't bother to ask about it or return them for further cooking. I knew that raw eggs can be a source for *Salmonella* and are risky to eat, but these were at least partially cooked and I had eaten scrambled eggs here many times before without ever contracting such a nasty bug. . . .

Thinking back to the severe cramps, diarrhea, headache, chills and slight fever, I realized how this disease could kill a child, elderly person or someone already ill or immune-compromised. I am a relatively young healthy adult and this thing turned me into a weak lump of flesh. All strength and energy was drained from me.

Physically, I am fully recovered, but in other ways I'm not the same. I am now much more aware of what to look for, or look out for, not just in a restaurant, but markets and even at home.

GLOSSARY

antibiotic A chemical that kills microorganisms and is used to fight bacterial infections.

bacteria Single-celled microorganisms; many common food-borne diseases are caused by bacteria.

botulism A rare but potentially fatal food-borne disease caused by the *Clostridium botulinum* bacterium, which grows in oxygen-free conditions, such as canned goods.

bovine spongiform encephalopathy (BSE) A neurodegenerative, invariably fatal disease of cattle caused by prions (malformed proteins). Humans eating meat from BSE-infected cattle may contract variant Creutzfeldt-Jakob disease.

Campylobacter A genus of bacterium that is a common cause of food-borne disease.

cold pasteurization The partial sterilization of food through irradiation or microfiltration.

cross-contamination The transfer of disease-causing microorganisms or other dangerous material to food through contact from unclean hands, utensils, another food, a cutting surface, etc.

***E. coli* O157:H7** One of the most harmful strains of *Escherichia coli* bacteria, *E. coli* O157:H7 contains a shigalike toxin and can cause kidney failure and death, especially in young children.

ergotism A disease caused by ingestion of toxins produced by *Claviceps purpurea* fungus, or ergot, which has infected wheat or other grains.

***Escherichia coli* (*E. coli*)** A type of bacteria normally found in the intestines of humans and other animals. It is usually harmless, but some strains can be deadly.

fungus Plantlike organisms such as mold or mushrooms; many can be a source of food-borne diseases, e.g., when a fungus infects a food crop.

gastroenteritis	Inflammation of the stomach and intestines, often caused by eating contaminated food or water, resulting in acute diarrhea and/or vomiting.
hepatitis A	A viral infection, often transmitted by contaminated food or water, that causes liver inflammation.
hemolytic uremic syndrome (HUS)	A serious complication of some food-borne diseases (particularly *E. coli* O157:H7) that can cause kidney failure or neurological damage.
irradiation	A method of reducing or eliminating pests and pathogens from food by exposing it to radiation; sometimes referred to as cold pasteurization.
Listeria	A type of food-borne bacteria that causes a gastrointestinal illness in humans.
microfiltration	A method of filtering microorganisms from liquids by passing them under pressure through a barrier with very tiny pores; sometimes referred to as cold pasteurization.
microorganisms	Any microscopic organism, such as bacteria, viruses, etc.
mycotoxin	A poison produced by a mold, mushroom, or other fungus.
Norwalk virus	One of the most common food-borne viral infections, Norwalk virus causes acute gastroenteritis.
parasite	An organism that lives on or in a host organism, deriving nourishment from the host without killing or benefiting the host.
pasteurization	A process of heating food in order to destroy harmful bacteria, without significantly altering the chemistry of the food.
pathogen	An infectious disease–producing agent such as a bacterium, virus, or prion.
prion	A toxic protein particle, believed to be the cause of variant Creutzfeldt-Jakob disease and bovine spongiform encephalopathy.
radiolytic products	New chemical products that are produced by the irradiation of food.

Salmonella	A rod-shaped bacterium that can cause typhoid fever and food poisoning.
shiga toxin	A deadly poison produced by some food-borne disease micro-organisms.
toxin	A poisonous substance produced by living cells or organisms, including bacteria in food.
variant Creutzfeldt-Jakob disease (vCJD)	A rare and invariably fatal neurodegenerative disease believed to be caused by prions in contaminated meat, particularly the meat of BSE-infected cattle.
virulence	The measure of how harmful a microorganism is.
virus	A microscopic organism that can only reproduce within the cells of other organisms; e.g. Norwalk virus and Hanta virus.
zoonoses	Diseases that normally affect animals but can be transmitted to humans; food-borne zoonotic diseases include *E. coli* O157:H7, *Campylobacter*, and *Salmonella*.

CHRONOLOGY

B.C.	6000	Neolithic humans, having developed agriculture, start preserving food for later consumption by cooling and salting it.
	750–687	The kosher dietary laws in the Bible's book of Leviticus offer some protection against food-borne diseases.
A.D.	1202	King John of England proclaims the first English food law, making it illegal to sell adulterated bread.
	1266–1267	The "Assize of Bread and Ale" bans British merchants from using chalk instead of flour.
	1822	*A Treatise on Adulteration of Food and Culinary Poisons* by Frederick C. Marcus reports that many common foods are adulterated.
	1862	President Abraham Lincoln establishes the US Department of Agriculture (USDA).
	1864	French chemist Louis Pasteur invents a process ("pasteurization") for killing harmful microorganisms in food and drink using heat.
	1872	England passes the Adulteration of Food or Drink Act, creating harsh penalties for adding contaminants to food or drink.
	1883	Scientists develop methods to detect adulteration of food; Dr. Harvey W. Wiley becomes chief chemist in the USDA's Division of Chemistry, and shifts its focus to the labeling of foods and beverages.

1891   The first comprehensive list of animal and human parasites is developed.

1902   Dr. Wiley creates a "Poison Squad" to test potentially harmful food additives on human volunteers.

1906   Upton Sinclair's book *The Jungle* is published, describing widespread unsanitary practices in the meat-processing industry. The resulting public outcry leads to passage in the United States of the Pure Food and Drug Act and the Meat Inspection Act later that year.

1910   Pasteurization is shown to destroy toxin-producing microorganisms in raw milk without killing beneficial lactic acid bacteria.

1915   Accused of unknowingly spreading typhus for years while working as a cook, Mary Mallon, dubbed "Typhoid Mary," is quarantined on North Brother Island until her death in 1938.

1928   Sir Alexander Fleming discovers that penicillin mold has antibacterial properties.

1930   The USDA's Bureau of Chemistry is renamed the Food and Drug Administration (FDA).

1940s   Irradiation of various foods is tested by the U.S. Army.

Early 1950s   Farmers start giving subtherapeutic doses of antibiotics to livestock to enhance growth.

1954   The Miller Amendment to the Federal Food, Drug, and Cosmetic Act is passed, permitting the FDA to establish acceptable levels of pesticides on agricultural products.

1957   The world's first commercial food irradiation occurs in Stuttgart, Germany.

1958   The FDA is allowed to ban food additives that have not been adequately tested for safety.

Late 1950s   The Hazard Analysis and Critical Control Points (HACCP) system is developed by the Pillsbury Corporation, working under contract to the National Aeronautics and Space Administration (NASA); its original purpose is to protect astronauts from food-borne diseases.

1960s   Japanese scientists determine that antibiotic resistance can be transferred between different types of bacteria; e.g., penicillin resistance can pass from *Salmonella* to *Campylobacter*.

1963   The FDA approves irradiation for wheat and wheat powder to control insects.

1970   The Environmental Protection Agency is formed and takes over regulation of pesticides.

1971   The HACCP system begins to be promoted outside of NASA.

1982   Prions, a new infectious agent, are discovered and proposed as a cause of transmissible spongiform encephalopathy diseases such as variant Creutzfeldt-Jakob disease.

1983   Irradiation to kill bacteria and insects in food spices and seasonings is approved by the FDA.

1984   In Oregon, followers of the guru Bhagwan Shree Rajneesh contaminate salad bars with *Salmonella*, resulting in almost eight hundred illnesses.

1985   A *Salmonella* outbreak caused by improperly pasteurized milk sickens two-hundred thousand people and kills four; one of the first large-scale *Listeria* outbreaks kills eighteen and results in an additional thirty still-births and infant deaths.

1985   Nearly a thousand people in Canada and the western United States are poisoned by residue of the pesticide Temik in watermelons.

1986   The first cases of bovine spongiform encephalopathy (BSE), known popularly as "mad cow disease," are diagnosed in Britain.

1986   Food irradiation is approved for fruits and vegetables by the FDA.

1993   An *E. coli* O157:H7 outbreak in Jack in the Box restaurants sickens over seven hundred people and kills four children.

1997   After sixteen people get ill from eating *E. coli* O157:H7–contaminated hamburger patties, 25 million pounds of hamburger are recalled.

1999   The National Academy of Sciences issues a warning that use of antibiotics in cattle feed increases the prevalence of antibiotic-resistant bacteria in humans.

2000   Irradiated beef becomes available.

2003   The first case of bovine spongiform encephalopathy (BSE) on US soil is confirmed.

2004   The FDA requires detailed record-keeping for all food so that the source of any bioterrorism outbreak can be determined.

2006   A multistate outbreak of *E. coli* in bagged spinach occurs, sickening hundreds of people.

2006   The FDA allows a bacteriophage (a virus that attacks and mutates bacteria) to be used in packaged foods to combat *Listeria*.

2007   Bioniche, a Canadian biopharmaceutical company, reports that a bovine vaccine it had developed reduces *E. coli* O157:H7 by over 99 percent.

2009   The USDA grants a conditional license for the first *E. coli* O157:H7 vaccine for cattle in the United States.

ORGANIZATIONS TO CONTACT

The editors have compiled the following list of organizations concerned with the issues debated in this book. The descriptions are derived from materials provided by the organizations. All have publications or information available for interested readers. The list was compiled on the date of publication of the present volume; the information provided here may change. Be aware that many organizations take several weeks or longer to respond to inquiries, so allow as much time as possible.

American Council on Science and Health (ACSH)
1995 Broadway, 2nd Fl.
New York, NY
10023-5860
phone: (212) 362-7044
fax: (212) 362-4919
e-mail: acsh@acsh.org
website: www.acsh.org

The ACSH provides consumers with scientific evaluations of food and the environment, pointing out both health hazards and benefits. It participates in a variety of government and media events and produces a wide range of publications, including the website HealthFactsAndFears.com, peer-reviewed reports on important health and environmental topics, and a semi-annual review of ACSH press coverage called "Media Update."

Biotechnology Industry Organization (BIO)
1201 Maryland Ave. SW, Ste. 900
Washington, DC
20024
phone: (202) 962-9200
fax: (202) 488-6301
e-mail: info@bio.org
website: www.bio.org

BIO represents biotechnology companies, academic institutions, and state biotechnology centers engaged in the development of products and services in the areas of biomedicine, agriculture, and environmental applications. The organization conducts workshops and produces educational materials aimed at increasing public understanding of biotechnology. The publications page on its website offers a variety of downloadable materials.

Center for Science in the Public Interest (CSPI)
1875 Connecticut Ave. NW, Ste. 300
Washington, DC 20009
phone: (202) 332-9110
fax: (202) 265-4954
e-mail: cspi@cspinet .org
website: www.cspinet .org

The CSPI is a nonprofit education and advocacy organization committed to improving the safety and nutritional quality of the US food supply. It publishes *Nutrition Action Healthletter*, the largest-circulation health newsletter in the country.

Food and Drug Administration (FDA)
10903 New Hampshire Ave.
Silver Spring, MD 20993-0002
phone: (888) 463-6332
e-mail: webmail@oc .fda.gov
website: www.fda.gov

The FDA is a public health agency, charged with protecting American consumers by enforcing the Federal Food, Drug, and Cosmetic Act and several related public health laws. To carry out this mandate of consumer protection, the FDA has investigators and inspectors covering the country's almost ninety-five thousand FDA-regulated businesses. Its publications include government documents, reports, fact sheets, and press announcements.

Food Safety and Inspection Service (FSIS)
US Department of Agriculture (USDA)
1400 Independence Ave. SW
Washington, DC 20250-3700
phone: (888) 674-6854
e-mail: fsiswebmaster@ usda.gov
website: www.fsis.usda .gov

The FSIS is the public health agency of the USDA that is responsible for ensuring that the nation's commercial supply of meat, poultry, and egg products is safe, wholesome, and correctly labeled and packaged. It publishes fact sheets, reports, articles, and brochures on food safety topics.

Food Safety Consortium (FSC)
110 Agriculture Bldg.
University of Arkansas
Fayetteville, AR 72701
phone: (479) 575-5647
fax: (479) 575-7531
e-mail: fsc@cavern.uark
.edu
website: www.uark.edu
/depts/fsc

Congress established the FSC, consisting of researchers from the University of Arkansas, Iowa State University, and Kansas State University, in 1988 through a special Cooperative State Research Service grant. The consortium conducts extensive investigation into all areas of poultry, beef, and pork production and publishes the quarterly *FSC Newsletter*.

FoodSafety.gov
US Department of
Health and Human
Services
200 Independence
Ave. SW
Washington, DC
20201
phone: (800) CDC-
INFO (232-4636)
website: www.food
safety.gov

FoodSafety.gov is the gateway to food safety information provided by US government agencies, including the Food and Drug Administration (FDA) and the Centers for Disease Control and Prevention (CDC). The website offers information on various food safety and foodborne disease–related topics, as well as offering an "Ask the Experts" section where food safety experts are available to answer questions via phone, e-mail, or live online chat.

International Vegetarian Union (IVU)
PO Box 4921
Washington, DC
20008
website: www.ivu.org

The IVU is a nonprofit organization that advocates animal welfare, humanitarian, and health objectives. It makes available on its website articles concerning food safety and issues from affiliate vegetarian organizations.

Organic Consumers Association (OCA)
6771 S. Silver Hill Dr.
Finland, MN 55603
phone: (218) 226-4164
fax: (218) 353-7652
website: www.organic
consumers.org

The OCA is a grassroots nonprofit public interest organization that deals with crucial issues of food safety, industrial agriculture, genetic engineering, corporate accountability, and environmental sustainability. The association publishes the newsletters *Organic View* and *Organic Bytes*, as well as fact sheets such as "Hazards of G.E. Foods and Crops."

Safe Tables Our Priority (S.T.O.P.)
3149 Dundee Rd. #276
Northbrook, IL 60062
phone: (847) 831-3032
fax: (847) 831-3032
e-mail: mail@safe
tables.org
website: www.safe
tables.org

S.T.O.P. is a nonprofit organization devoted to victim assistance, public education, and policy advocacy for safe food and public health. S.T.O.P.'s mission is to prevent unnecessary illness and loss of life from pathogenic foodborne illness. S.T.O.P.'s publications include newsletters, policy statements, testimonies, and press releases.

World Health Organization (WHO)
Avenue Appia 20
1211 Geneva 27
Switzerland
phone: + 41 22 791
21 11
fax: + 41 22 791 31 11
website: www.who
.int/en/

WHO is the directing and coordinating authority for health within the United Nations system. It is responsible for providing leadership on global health matters, shaping the health research agenda, setting norms and standards, articulating evidence-based policy options, providing technical support to countries and monitoring and assessing health trends. Its website contains information on foodborne diseases as well as many other global health problems.

FOR FURTHER READING

Books

Madeline Drexler, *Emerging Epidemics: The Menace of New Infections.* London: Penguin, 2010.

Sari Edelstein, *Food and Nutrition at Risk in America: Food Insecurity, Biotechnology, Food Safety and Bioterrorism.* Boston: Jones & Bartlett, 2008.

Jonathan A. Edlow, *The Deadly Dinner Party: And Other Medical Detective Stories.* New Haven, CT: Yale University Press, 2009.

Phyllis Entis, *Food Safety: Old Habits and New Perspectives.* Washington, DC: ASM Press, 2007.

Beatrice Trum Hunter, *Infectious Connections: How Short-Term Foodborne Infections Can Lead to Long-Term Health Problems.* Laguna Beach, CA: Basic Health, 2009.

Christine Little and Jim McLauchlin, eds., *Hobbs' Food Poisoning and Food Hygiene.* 7th ed. London: Hodder Arnold, 2007.

Michele Morrone, *Poisons on Our Plates: The Real Food Safety Problem in the United States.* Westport, CT: Praeger, 2008.

Marion Nestle, *Safe Food: The Politics of Food Safety.* 2nd ed. Berkeley and Los Angeles: University of California Press, 2010.

Robyn O'Brien, *The Unhealthy Truth: One Mother's Shocking Investigation into the Dangers of America's Food Supply—and What Every Family Can Do to Protect Itself.* New York: Broadway Books, 2009.

Michael Pollan, *The Omnivore's Dilemma: The Secrets Behind What You Eat.* Young Reader's Ed. New York: Dial Books, 2009.

Nina E. Redman, *Food Safety.* 2nd ed. Santa Barbara, CA: ABC-CLIO, 2007.

Paul Roberts, *The End of Food.* New York: Houghton Mifflin Harcourt, 2008.

Morton Satin, *Death in the Pot: The Impact of Food Poisoning on History.* Amherst, NY: Prometheus Books, 2007.

————, *Food Alert! The Ultimate Sourcebook for Food Safety.* New York: Checkmark Books, 2008.

Ian Shaw, *Is It Safe to Eat? Enjoy Eating and Minimize Food Risks.* New York: Springer, 2005.

Carl Zimmer, *Microcosm: E. Coli and the New Science of Life.* New York: Pantheon Books, 2008.

Periodicals and Internet Sources

Holly Auer, "Planes, Trains & Pains," *Charleston (SC) Post and Courier,* June 18 2007.

Brita Belli, "Nuking Food: Contamination Fears and Market Possibilities Spur an Irradiation Revival," *E: The Environmental Magazine,* July–Aug. 2007.

Rebecca Berg, "'I Just Don't Want Them Doing That to My Food': The Backlash Against Science and Its Implications for Environmental Health," *Journal of Environmental Health,* vol. 71, no. 4, 2008.

Linda Brandt, "Bacteria Isn't the Enemy," *Sarasota (FL) Herald Tribune,* February 24, 2010.

Kristin Choo, "Hungry for Change: The Feds Consider a Steady Diet of Stronger Regulation to Help Fix the US Food Safety Network," *ABA Journal,* vol. 95, no. 9, 2009.

Alan Pell Crawford, "Fly-by Food Terrorism," *Vegetarian Times,* February 2006.

Economist, "Disease and Intelligence: *Mens Sana in Corpore Sano*: Parasites and Pathogens May Explain Why People in Some Parts of the World Are Cleverer than Others, July 1, 2010. www.economist.com/node/16479286?story_id=16479286.

Richard Eshelman, "I Survived the 'Destroying Angel,'" *Cornell Mushroom Blog,* http://blog.mycology.cornell.edu/?p=68, November 22, 2006.

Kathy Freston, "*E. coli, Salmonella* and Other Deadly Bacteria and Pathogens in Food: Factory Farms Are the Reason," *Huffington Post,* January 8, 2010. www.huffingtonpost.com/kathy-freston/e-coli-salmonella-and-oth_b_415240.html.

Harvard Men's Health Watch, "Food-Borne Illnesses, Part I: The Big Picture," March 1, 2010.

————, "Food-Borne Illnesses, Part II: Personal Protection, April 1, 2010.

Karen Kaplan, "The Science of *Salmonella*," *Los Angeles Times*, August 10, 2009. http://articles.latimes.com/2009/aug/10/health/he-salmonella10.

Jim Kouri, "Danger: Food Supply Vulnerable to Terrorism," Mensnewsdaily.com, October 21, 2009. http://mensnewsdaily.com/2009/10/21/danger-food-supply-vulnerable-to-terrorism.

Paul Krugman, "Fear of Eating," *New York Times*, May 21, 2007.

Richard Laliberte, "Should We Fear Our Food? *Redbook*, May 2007.

Michael Moss, "The Burger that Shattered Her Life," *New York Times*, October 4, 2009.

Michael Pollan, "The Vegetable-Industrial Complex," *New York Times Magazine*, October 15, 2006.

Sonia Reyes, "Harvest of Fear," *Brandweek*, vol. 48, no. 10, 2007.

Kate Rope, "Diary of a Germophobe," *Shape*, November 2009.

Henry Samuel, "1951 mystery of the Cursed Bread Was a CIA Test with LSD, Says Writer," *Daily Telegraph* (London), March 11, 2010.

David Schardt, "Caution! Playing Russian Roulette with Your Food," *Nutrition Action Healthletter*, March 2010.

Jørgen Schlundt, "Food Safety Is Critical to Nutrition Security," SciDev.net, January 20, 2010. www.scidev.net/en/opinions/food-safety-is-critical-to-nutrition-security.html.

Adam Voiland, "The Basics on the Foodfight over Irradiation," *U.S. News & World Report*, September 5, 2008.

Elizabeth Weise and Julie Schmit, "Five Faces. Five Agonizing Deaths. One Year Later," *USA Today*, September 21, 2007.

Calvin Woodward, "On the Trail of a Killer," *Tampa (FL) Tribune*, February 14, 2009.

Carl Zimmer, "How Microbes Defend and Define Us," *New York Times*, July 13 2010.

INDEX

economic costs of, 28, *61, 75*
fears of, are exaggerated, 67–71
federal government is failing to protect
   people against, 72–78
finding source of, is difficult, 49–57
groups at high risk for, 63
is an increasing problem, 59–66
microorganisms causing, 18
most common, 19
outbreaks of, in schools, by type, *83*
prevalence of, 18, *19*, 26, 60
symptoms of, 28, 63–64
underreporting of, 65
See also specific diseases
Freese, Bill, 91, 93–94, 95

G
Gaul, Linda, 53
Genetically modified organisms (GMO),
   23
Government Accountability Office, US
   (GAO),
   76
Grassley, Charles, 88–89
Greaney, T.J., 67
Green Revolution, 85
Guillain-Barré syndrome, 64

H
Hallmark/Westland meat-packing plant,
   80, 83
Hazard analysis and critical control point
   (HACCP), 23
Hemolytic uremic syndrome (HUS),
   43–44, 64, 116
Hepatitis A virus, 22
Houk, Kimberlae, 50, 51–52, 53
Hunger, prevalence of, 85

I
Indian Health Service, 50–51, 53

Influenza virus, H1N1 (bird flu), 27
Inland Valley Daily Bulletin (newspaper),
   80
International Food Safety Forum (World
   Health Organization, 2007), *31*
Investigations
   of food-borne disease outbreaks, steps
      in, *54*
   of *Salmonella* outbreak, 49–53, 55–57
Irradiation. *See* Food irradiation

J
Jones, Vicky, 123
Journal of Food Production, 46, 82
Jungk, Jessica, 55

K
Kimbrell, Andrew, 72

L
Listeria monocytogenes, 62, 63–64
   listeriosis caused by, *21,* 21–22
localvore movement, 59, 71
LSD (lysergic acid diethylamide), 34

M
Mad cow disease. *See* Bovine spongiform
   encephalopathy
Madden, Alan, 119–122
Madden, Kate, 119–122
Markarian, Michael, 79
Marler, Bill, 96
Mead, Paul, 66
Meat production, 76
   E. coli O157:H7 infection and, 41–42
   use of antibiotics in, 13, 46
Mendell, Steve, *81*
Millennium Development Goals (MDGs),
   26, 28
MSNBC (TV channel), 99

personal account of mother losing son to, 118–122